Fight the Patriarchy
A Survival Guide

by

Nikki De Mars

Edited by Raya De Mars

Illustrated by Sarah Solomon

ISBN: 979-8-218-09143-9
EISBN: 979-8-218-09144-6

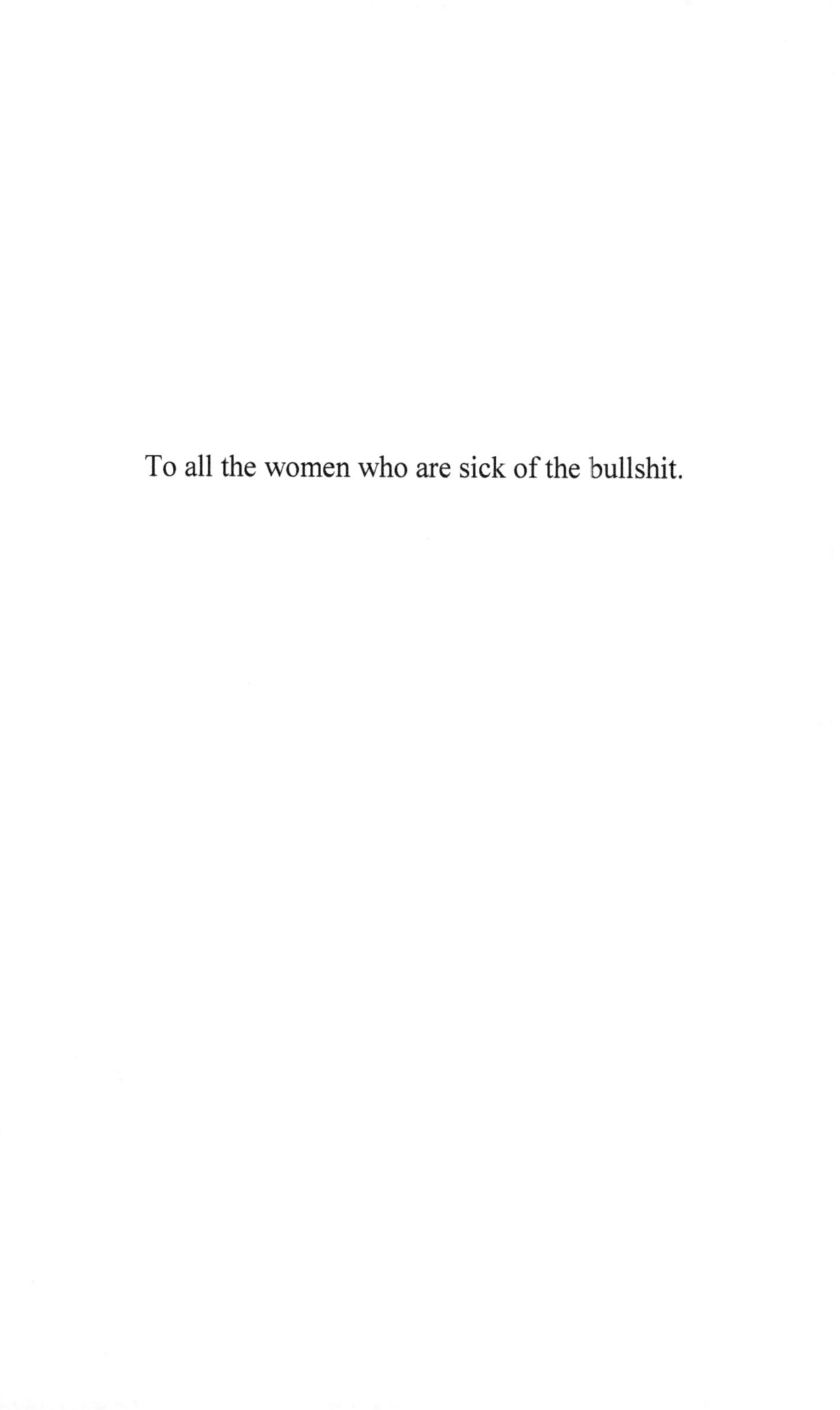

To all the women who are sick of the bullshit.

Contents

patriarchy (noun)

pa·tri·ar·chy | \ ˈpā-trē-ˌär-kē \
plural: patriarchies

Definition of patriarchy

1: social organization marked by the supremacy
of the father in the clan or family, the legal
dependence of wives and children, and the
reckoning of descent and inheritance in the male
line

broadly : control by men of a disproportionately
large share of power

2: a society or institution organized according to
the principles or practices of patriarchy
// For 20 years the country was ruled as a
patriarchy.[1]

---

[1] Merriam-Webster, *Patriarchies Definition & Meaning.*

On Friday, June 24th, 2022, at 7:36 a.m. I awoke to the familiar "ding" of a text message. The message was from my soon-to-be ex-husband, who was working in another state at the time. It read, "Roe v Wade was overturned." My mouth became as dry as a cotton ball. Boiling fury burned in the pit of my stomach, then exploded through my veins. My limbs throbbed and tingled with pure hatred for all the people who had fought to steal away women's unalienable right to sovereignty over their bodies. I spent the next three days alternating between rage and hopelessness. I could not believe the audacity of the religious zealots who had infiltrated our government, including the highest court in the land, and rammed their beliefs down millions of Americans' throats.

I felt betrayed by the Supreme Court, the American government, and friends and family members who voted for Trump and continued to advocate for the rights of fetuses over women's rights. A central tenet of Trump's 2016 presidential campaign was that states have the final say on abortion laws within their jurisdiction. Trump promised over and over to appoint pro-life federal judges and justices to the Supreme Court. On the national stage of the presidential debate held on October 19, 2016, he stated, "Well, if we put another two or perhaps three justices on, that's really what's going to be—that will happen. And that'll happen automatically, in my opinion, because I am putting pro-life justices on the court. I will say this: It will go back to the states, and the states will then make a determination."[2] Despite Trump's blatant disregard for women's rights, 62,985,106 people voted for this despicable man.[3] I was scared for my daughter and nieces, who would grow up in a world where their physical and mental health and possibly even their lives would be inconsequential if they ever got pregnant. I was angry for all the men and women who had sacrificed their lives for Americans to be free. For the Supreme Court to rip away the right to control your own body and choose your destiny from half the population was a slap in those service members' faces. I was in disbelief that I was no longer a full-fledged citizen of my country, the country I loved and had served. I no longer had the same rights as a man. I no longer had a right to personal autonomy or equal protection under the law. I could not understand how this could happen in the United States of America.

The shock of this new, insane reality that Conservatives had forced women into eventually began to wear off, but the

---

[2] The Commission on Presidential Debates, *October 19, 2016 Debate Transcript.*
[3] The New York Times, *2016 Presidential Election Results.*

anger remained, and I'm glad it did. My anger gave me the energy and motivation to stop sulking around and instead begin formulating a plan. It all boils down to this: right-wing extremists obliterated the protection of the unenumerated rights of privacy and personal autonomy that had protected women from governmental overreach. These rights did not just protect women. They safeguarded men who wanted to use a condom because they weren't ready for a child. They protected homosexuals who wanted to be free to be intimate with their loved ones in the privacy of their own homes. They protected any Americans who held beliefs contrary to the prevailing opinions of their time. This is not an exhaustive list of privacy rights, but it demonstrates the breadth of what right-wing extremists have taken away.

I'm afraid of what the future holds for all Americans. If we are willing to compromise the rights of one group, what will keep us from taking rights from the next? The decision in Dobbs v. Jackson Women's Health Organization to overturn the precedent set by Roe v. Wade will have far-reaching effects on American society, not just on women. All Americans who recognize the danger of this decision and believe in equal rights and freedoms for all people must stand up and fight this despicable judgment with ferocity. If we are complacent, there will be no freedom for future generations of Americans. We are at a turning point in our nation's history and must rise to the occasion.

At the root of the Supreme Court's decision to overturn Roe v. Wade is the political ideology of Christian Nationalism (currently synonymous with the MAGA, or Make America Great Again, movement), which is both intertwined and coextensive with patriarchal ideology. Christian Nationalism is a set of beliefs rooted in the idea that the forefathers founded the United States as a Christian nation. Therefore, the government should be guided by Christian principles. Furthermore, the government should actively work to maintain this status quo. Specific to the current brand of Christian Nationalism in the United States is the belief that Christians must embrace traditional family structures and hierarchies as well as conventional gender roles. It's no secret that Christianity, as well as other major religions, is rooted in patriarchy. God is a father figure, Jesus is a man, and men run the church and make the rules. Conservative Christian society also sees men as the head of the family unit. They see women, like Mary, as nothing more than vessels for bringing forth more men. They reward women for being "pure" and obedient. Women bear and rear children and take care of the home and the cooking so that men can be more comfortable.

Similar ideologies are overrunning countries, such as Afghanistan and Iran, in the Middle East, where Islamism, a form of Muslim nationalism, has roots. In Islamism again exists the interweaving of religion with patriarchal ideology. These religions can and do exist without patriarchy. Religious leaders and their followers at many churches, synagogues, and mosques fight against traditional patriarchal ideas. A person can believe in the basic teachings of religion without embracing its traditional cultural components. The force at the center of Christian Nationalism is the patriarchy. Religion is merely the vehicle by which the patriarchy attempts to exert control. Therefore, Americans' quarrel should not be with religion but with those in the patriarchy who are exploiting it. We must banish this ideology from Americans' hearts, minds, and institutions if our democracy is to endure.

The idea that the people agree to be governed in exchange for government protection of their human rights is a founding principle in our democracy. The most basic principle of patriarchy is that women are not equal to men. Women are subservient to men and therefore do not enjoy the same rights. A government that does not protect the human rights of half of its population is asking for a revolution. Women will not continue to submit to a government that does not hold up its end of the bargain. I hope that men will not either.

I wrote this book not as a roadmap for existing in a patriarchal society but as a roadmap for conquering and overcoming a patriarchal society. I wrote from the female perspective and to a female audience because we have shared experiences. However, these suggestions can be helpful to anyone fighting the patriarchy, despite their difference in experience from women. I recognize that women are not the only people suppressed by patriarchal systems. I hope all groups, including men who acknowledge the system's malfeasance, will join this battle. In August of 2022, in defense of his view that abortion should be illegal regardless of whether or not the mother's life is in jeopardy, John Jacobs (a Republican in the State of Indiana House of Representatives) said, "The body inside of the mom's body is not her body. Let me repeat that: The body inside of the mom's body is not her body. Not her body, not her choice."[4] This callous disregard for women's lives cannot stand in our country. We cannot go down this road. If America is going to survive, we must dismantle the scourge of patriarchy. It is a system of dominance of one group over the many. It is the antithesis of freedom. I hope this guide will give all Americans some ideas on what they can do

---

[4] Scribner, *'Not Her Body, Not Her Choice': Indiana Legislature Passes near-Total Abortion Ban.*

to fight the patriarchy and ensure the survival of our great nation.

CHAPTER ONE
Why This Mission Matters

What does the future look like for my daughter and nieces? Will 50% of the population be able to get the medical care they need? When the Supreme Court took away the right to an abortion, it opened a can of worms with far-reaching consequences. Currently, women are on the receiving end of the Court's overreach. Women across the country who live in red states are having difficulty getting misoprostol (used to protect against stomach ulcers[5]) and mifepristone[6] (used to treat uterine leiomyomas and Cushing's syndrome[7]). The combination of these two medications is the only pharmaceutical treatment for miscarriage in the first trimester.[8] Yet, they have been labeled abortion-inducing drugs by states such as Texas.[9]

Abortion bans are causing the availability of these drugs to be extremely limited and harming women's health, the extent of which we will not understand for years to come. In October of 2022, a pregnant woman in Texas was told her fetus was not viable but that abortion was not an option due to Texas's new

---

[5] WebMD, *Misoprostol-Uses, Side Effects, and More.*
[6] Kimball, *Women in states that ban abortion will still be able to get abortion pills online from overseas.*
[7] Autry and Wadhwa, *Mifepristone.*
[8] Huff, *In Texas, Abortion Laws Inhibit Care for Miscarriages.*
[9] Huff, *In Texas, Abortion Laws Inhibit Care for Miscarriages.*

abortion law.[10] Texas law bans abortion after only six weeks of gestation with the only exception being to save the life of the mother.[11] Texas also imposes severe criminal consequences on providers who perform abortions after six weeks.[12] Since the woman's life was not in imminent danger, doctors sent her home to wait for her body to miscarry naturally.[13] Rather than miscarrying she nearly died from an infection, had to have a subsequent surgery to remove scar tissue from her uterus, and now may not be able to carry children in the future.[14] Doctors and pharmacists fear providing these drugs or performing abortions, even when the woman's life could be threatened, for fear of prosecution by the state.

According to An International Journal of Obstetrics and Gynaecology, one out of three hundred women will not discover an abnormality in their fetus until their third-trimester scan.[15] Under restrictive abortion laws likely to be enacted in

---

[10] Bahari, *Texas woman nearly died from infection because doctors could not perform legal abortion.*

[11] ACLU, *Abortion in Texas.*

[12] ACLU, *Abortion in Texas.*

[13] Bahari, *Texas woman nearly died from infection because doctors could not perform legal abortion.*

[14] Bahari, *Texas woman nearly died from infection because doctors could not perform legal abortion.*

[15] Drukker et al., *How Often Do We Identify Fetal Abnormalities during Routine Third-Trimester Ultrasound? A Systematic Review and Meta-Analysis,* 259-269.

26 U.S. states, women in the third trimester would have no option but to carry these pregnancies to term, whether or not their fetus is viable. As I write this book, state laws are constantly changing in reaction to the Supreme Court's decision to overturn Roe v. Wade. So far, several states have severely limited abortion access and have made no exception for rape or incest. This, to me, is tantamount to both psychological and physical torture. I can't express how disgusted I am at the lack of rights women now have over their bodies and the lack of medical care that women are already experiencing. I believe women's prospects will only become grimmer as states continue to enact more restrictive abortion laws.

Another consequence of the Court's detrimental decision to reject women's right to govern their bodies is that women are now even more at risk of prosecution for pregnancy outcomes. A 2013 study found 413 cases where women had been detained for a crime connected to their pregnancy.[16] National Advocates for Pregnant Women recorded 1,331 of these cases between 2006 and 2020.[17] Women have been

---

[16] Paltrow and Flavin, *Arrests of and Forced Interventions on Pregnant Women in the United States, 1973–2005: Implications for Women's Legal Status and Public Health.*
[17] National Advocates for Pregnant Women, *Arrests and Prosecutions of Pregnant Women, 1973-2020.*

charged with murder for suffering stillbirths, attempting suicide while pregnant, and even for having a miscarriage after falling down a flight of stairs.[18] Many states are currently trying to grant fetuses personhood. The repercussions will be that states will investigate miscarriages and stillbirths as possible homicides. If a fetus is a person, then its death must be examined. These intrusions will open women up to criminal probes during one of the most trying times of their lives. This ruling will result in women going to prison not only for abortions but also for miscarriages. I am frightened for my daughter.

The Supreme Court's decision will have significant economic consequences as well. According to the Guttmacher Institute, 73% of women seeking abortions do so because they cannot afford to have a baby.[19] If the government denies women access to abortion, it will force more women out of the labor force, and women's overall earnings will decrease while their levels of poverty and debt increase.[20] The Supreme Court has seriously hindered women's ability to determine their

---

[18] Goodwin, *How the Criminalization of Pregnancy Robs Women of Reproductive Autonomy.*

[19] Finer et al., *Reasons U.S. Women Have Abortions: Quantitative and Qualitative Perspectives,* 110-118.

[20] Durkee, *Overturning Roe v. Wade: Here's How Abortion Bans Will Hurt State Economies and the GDP.*

financial future and has increased the financial burden that will fall on state welfare systems.

The decision of Roe v. Wade hinged on the idea that the 14th Amendment to the Constitution's Due Process Clause provides a right to privacy. The 14th Amendment states:

All persons born or naturalized in the United States, and subject to the jurisdiction thereof, are citizens of the United States and of the state wherein they reside. No state shall make or enforce any law which shall abridge the privileges or immunities of citizens of the United States; nor shall any state deprive any person of life, liberty, or property, without due process of law; nor deny to any person within its jurisdiction the equal protection of the laws.

The unenumerated right to privacy is linked to Americans' right to liberty, specifically spelled out in both the 14th and the 5th Amendments. The 5th Amendment specifies:

No person shall be held to answer for a capital, or otherwise infamous crime, unless on a presentment or indictment of a grand jury, except in cases arising in the land or naval forces, or in the militia, when in actual service in time of war or public danger; nor shall any person be subject for the same offense to be twice put in jeopardy of life or limb; nor shall be compelled in any criminal case to be a witness against himself, nor be deprived of life, liberty, or property, without due process of law; nor shall private property be taken for public use, without just compensation.

Furthermore, the 9th Amendment says, "The enumeration in the Constitution, of certain rights, shall not be construed to deny or disparage others retained by the people." This means that human rights exist whether or not they are spelled out in the Constitution.

The Universal Declaration of Human Rights states in Article 12, "No one shall be subjected to arbitrary interference with his privacy, family, home or correspondence, nor to attacks upon his honour and reputation. Everyone has the right to the protection of the law against such interference or attacks." Despite this, the Supreme Court's decision in Dobbs v. Jackson Women's Health Organization, the case in which they overturned the precedent set by Roe v. Wade, severely restricted American citizens' fundamental right to privacy. In this case, the Supreme Court upheld Mississippi's Gestational Age Act as constitutional. This act made it illegal to perform an abortion in Mississippi after 15 weeks of gestation unless it's a "medical emergency" or there is "severe fetal abnormality."[21] The Court completely disregarded The Universal Declaration of Human Rights which, by the way, has been recognized by 192 countries around the world,[22] three separate Amendments to the Constitution of the United States, and the precedent set by Roe v. Wade in 1973. The Supreme Court has no respect for the rule of law.

In his concurring opinion, Justice Clarence Thomas suggested that the Court reconsider other rights protected by the Constitution's unenumerated right to privacy. He wrote, "For that reason, in future cases, we should reconsider all of this Court's substantive due process precedents, including Griswold, Lawrence, and Obergefell."[23] The Griswold case upheld the right to contraception, Lawrence ruled that couples have a right to privacy in the bedroom (it got rid of sodomy laws), and Obergefell gave Americans a right to same-sex marriage. The precedent set by the Dobbs decision reaches much farther than women's right to an abortion. This court case could lead to women losing the right to decide whether or not

---

[21] Cornell Law School, *Dobbs v. Jackson Women's Health Organization.*
[22] Youth for Human Rights, *United Nations Universal Declaration of Human Rights.*
[23] Thomas, *Thomas E. Dobbs, State Health Officer of the Mississippi Department of Health, et al., Petitioners v. Jackson Women's Health Organization, et al.,* 119.

to get pregnant at all. It could lead to the government dictating how and with whom Americans can have sex. It could lead to same-sex couples losing their right to be legally recognized as married, the consequence of which could be a loss of health insurance, parental rights, and inheritance rights.

The preamble of our Constitution reads, "We the People of the United States, in Order to form a more perfect Union, establish Justice, insure domestic Tranquility, provide for the common defence, promote the general Welfare, and secure the Blessings of Liberty to ourselves and our Posterity, do ordain and establish this Constitution for the United States of America." Justice, domestic Tranquility, general Welfare, and the Blessing of Liberty are currently under attack by the patriarchy. America was founded on the ideal, "that all men are created equal, that they are endowed by their Creator with certain unalienable Rights, that among these are Life, Liberty and the pursuit of Happiness." The Supreme Court has stripped all three unalienable Rights from large segments of our population. There is a movement in our country to take these rights from all but white, Christian, heterosexual males. The people who support the patriarchy don't consider the rest of us part of the "men" referenced in the Declaration of Independence. They think we are "others" and therefore unworthy of the Constitution's protections.

The United States of America cannot be a free country unless ALL its citizens enjoy equal protection under the law. We outnumber the patriarchy, and we can overcome them. Make no mistake; we are at a turning point in American history. Every one of us has a significant role in deciding whether our nation moves boldly and openly toward freedom or retreats like cowards toward comfortable and antiquated traditions that will forever bar us from fully embracing liberty and equality for all people.

Your Mission

Piece by Piece,
Person by Person,
OBLITERATE THE PATRIARCHY

CHAPTER TWO
Rules for Nourishing Your Sanity

Rule 1: Celebrate Every Triumph!

If you're reading this book, you've probably already figured out how pervasively patriarchal ideas have infiltrated our society. You've probably realized that men aren't the only ones who espouse patriarchal ideations; women hold them just as deeply. You've probably concluded that we've all been brainwashed since birth to fit neatly into the patriarchal framework that makes up our society and nation. If you're anything like me, you want nothing more than to rip the patriarchal fabric of our society into tiny shreds and then stomp on them. You want to slap the faces of all the women who continue to wander the country with blinders on, complicit in their own subjugation. You want to throat-punch the men who wallow in the benefits of patriarchy, all while denying its existence. Well, I regretfully inform you that your frustrations are nowhere near an end. This mission, should you choose to accept it, is the dictionary definition of impossible.

impossible (adjective)

im·pos·si·ble | \ (ˌ)im-ˈpä-sə-bəl \

Definition of *impossible*

1 a: incapable of being or of occurring
b: felt to be incapable of being done, attained, or
fulfilled : insuperably difficult
// an *impossible* deadline

2 a: extremely undesirable : unacceptable
b: extremely awkward or difficult to deal with
// the actor was *impossible* on the set[24]

One person alone, even throughout an entire lifetime, is incapable of defeating the patriarchy, so don't delude yourself. You will not see the downfall of the patriarchy in your lifetime. It simply will not happen. The patriarchy's defeat will only come if generations of Americans set their minds to the grueling task of day by day, mind by mind, institution by institution, eradicating our nation of the injurious ideas, beliefs, and systems that have oppressed women, non-white people, and all who do not conform to traditional gender stereotypes for millennia. We will win our freedom from the scourge of patriarchy incrementally and over centuries (hopefully not millennia). By keeping in mind the monumental

---

[24] Merriam-Webster, *Impossible Definition & Meaning*.

size of the task of destroying the patriarchy, you will be able to safeguard your sanity. By realizing that you will never see the war won, you can keep your frustrations at the lack of change at bay.

I hope I haven't painted an overly bleak picture. I don't want you to despair. To say that you will not see the war won is not to say you won't see victory. There will be many, many battles along the way. Relish every triumph, no matter how small, for every tiny victory brings us one step closer to accomplishing our mission. Don't diminish the importance of every minute win. It's only through the accumulation of quadrillions of tiny victories that we will stamp out patriarchal ideology. That brings me to the rules for nourishing your sanity:

Rule 1: celebrate every triumph!

Rule 2: Take Breaks

Due to the omnipresent nature of patriarchy and the gargantuan size of the task of dismantling it, you will often be exhausted. You have been and will continue to be surrounded by people and systems that work to relegate you to your given place in the patriarchal hierarchy. You will have bosses who continuously judge you more harshly than your male counterparts. You will have co-workers and lovers whose expectations of you are both hypocritical and outrageous. You will be expected to uphold ridiculous, time-consuming standards of feminine beauty while maintaining a pristine house, raising children, and proving your commitment to work and career. You will be ignored or outright silenced in meetings. You will be told to be more assertive, only to be criticized for being "bitchy" when you speak up. You will have conversations with men and women who say they don't understand why you rail about women's rights and insist that patriarchy is a thing of the past.

This daily onslaught will wear you down. It will leave you drained and discouraged. You will feel as if your heart and courage have shrunk away and found a dark corner in which to hide. You must know that it's okay to take a rest. Go to a peaceful place for a while. Give yourself time to regain your strength. Sometimes you have to allow yourself to ignore, overlook, or forget the insults and frustration. Now and then, find your happy place, and don't let anyone or anything disturb you.

Rule 2: take breaks

Rule 3: Uncork Your Rage

Let's be honest; you will be angry at the slow incremental pace of change. You will be outraged at fathers who tell daughters, "You throw like a girl." You will be pissed at lovers who see you as an object to be owned and controlled. You will be irate at people who act shocked when you show competence at a task that is thought to be masculine. You will want to scream at sisters who engage in tearing down other women to elevate themselves. Women who claim they only hang out with men because women are too petty will make you want to tear your hair out. Americans who are overly critical of female politicians while they advocate for the most crooked men will make you want to vomit. Scorching hot rage will sear you from the inside out, spreading from your burning bowels to your fiery heart and out through your nerves to your red-hot fingers and toes. You will want to explode. You will need to relieve the building pressure.

Let. It. Out. Find a group of like-minded women and have a fucking pity party. Rant and rave about the unfairness of it all. Throw all the jerks who've pissed you off under the bus, and don't worry about how bad it makes them look. Go on social media and let your anger be known. Blow up at a co-worker and name them for the sexist they are. Go to a protest and scream and yell. Tell your mom her beliefs are antiquated and detrimental to women's equality. Sometimes, you must say what needs to be said and not hold back. Sometimes, you have to let it off your chest and give people a good dose of your reality. Don't hold it in, or it will eat you alive. Let your rage explode from you. Set it free into the world.

Rule 3: uncork your rage

Rule 4: Pick Your Battles

As with any war, there is a cost to doing battle. When you make public statements on Twitter, you risk being ridiculed and disparaged by people who disagree with you. When you confront a co-worker, you risk being labeled the workplace troublemaker. When you disagree with a family member, you risk damaging the relationship. There will be times when the cost of doing battle is too high. It's okay to sit those battles out.

It's up to each of us, individually, to determine which battles we can wage and which ones we cannot. We already have a lot of people on our side. There is another person, possibly multiple people, in a better position to fight that battle than you are. For example, if you're a single mother and your kids will go hungry if you lose your job, the possible cost of pointing out to your boss that he has a sexist attitude is probably too high. That is a battle that you might choose to leave for someone else to fight. Surely that man has friends or siblings that should be confronting him. In another case, you may have an extremely conservative father who refuses to consider other points of view or who refuses to be questioned by his child. The cost of pointing out flaws in his logic may be higher than you're willing to pay. It could cost you a meaningful relationship in your life. Sometimes, you must safeguard your financial, social, or emotional well-being, even if that means forgoing a battle here and there.

I don't want you to construe this as kicking the can down the road or leaving problems for others to handle. If you see something wrong, you should say or do something. You should fight every battle you can, large and small. When conducting your cost-benefit analysis, you should also consider how egregious the behavior or issue is. Sometimes, the cost of ignoring behavior will be much higher than the cost of confronting it. For example, if your boss inappropriately touches someone, that is far different than if your boss tends to ask women to make coffee in the morning. Neither is appropriate. Neither is acceptable. If I had mouths to feed, I would put making coffee at the bottom of my list of battles to fight or be very strategic in how I address it. You have to give yourself and your allies the space to decide as individuals whether or not you can handle the consequences of a particular battle. This is a war of attrition. The only way to win is to convert one person at a time. You must be in this for the long haul. You have to be able to pay your bills. You have to have the option of maintaining familial relationships that are important to you. You cannot go into this war thinking you'll give all or nothing. Patriarchal ideas are so pervasive in our society that if you give all, you will have nothing left. Give what you can, rest, regroup, and then get back into the fight.

Rule 4: pick your battles

CHAPTER THREE
Get LOUD!!!

Argue, Argue, Argue

I'm sure you've heard the adage, "Arguing with a fool only proves that there are two." Ignore that. You must argue with ALL the fools. Fools are generally good, well-meaning people. However, they've drunk the patriarchal Kool-aid and haven't yet emerged from their drunken, delusional stupor. The only way to extricate them from its power is to ply them with logical arguments and facts in the hope that they can see the light and reemerge as a rational and perceptive person. Most of us can sympathize as we have also been fools at some point in our lives (I know I have). We are constantly gaining new knowledge and being exposed to different perspectives, which should prompt us to grow and change our way of thinking. I'm sure, in some ways, I'm still a fool waiting for someone to pull me out of the Kool-Aid. Some fools, however, are submerged more deeply in the Kool-Aid than others and will be more challenging to reach, but we must try. Every person pulled from its powerful grip is one small battle won, one more ally, and one less drop in the bucket of patriarchal power. Each fool we can rip from the grasp of the patriarchy will have exponential effects in the future. A mother turned from her shackles will teach her sons and daughters to believe in and fight for equality for all. A man awakened to his privilege will work to level the playing field in the future. Please, argue with fools.

As you undertake this mission, you will need some tools to guide you. First of all, you must always ensure that your arguments are logical. I firmly believe that, over time, logic and reason can wear down the most staunch and combative of fools. To ensure the logic of your arguments, I'd like to provide you with a list of fallacies to avoid. I find it helpful to review these from time to time, not only so that I can avoid using them, but also so that I can point them out for what they are when fools use them. Below is a list of logical fallacies to eschew.

- ad hominem: when someone attacks the person making an argument instead of the argument itself

- straw man: when someone attacks a hyperbolic or distorted version of someone's argument

- red herring: when someone interjects an irrelevant point or idea to shift the focus of the argument

- slippery slope: when someone claims, without evidence, that another person's idea will lead to a series of undesirable or extreme events

- appeal to authority: when someone claims something is true because a supposed expert said so

- appeal to ignorance: when someone claims something is true merely because it hasn't been proven to be false

- appeal to pity: when someone tries to get you to agree with their argument by stirring up strong emotions

- bandwagon: when someone claims something is true or claims it's a good thing simply because a lot of people agree with it

- circular argument: when someone's conclusion is the same thing as their premise (example: abortion is immoral because I believe it is sinful)

- false dilemma: when someone claims there are only two options to fix a problem and that no other solutions exist

- appeal to hypocrisy: when someone claims that your argument is false because you don't behave in accordance with your own beliefs

- appeal to tradition: when someone claims that something is a good thing or is true because people have been doing it or have believed it for a long time

- hasty generalization: when someone makes a statement based on evidence drawn from a tiny sample

- sunk cost fallacy: when someone uses the amount of time or money that has been spent on something as justification for not changing course

- causal fallacy: when someone claims that one thing causes another without evidence that the relationship actually exists

I genuinely believe most Americans who inadvertently support the patriarchy believe in freedom and equal rights for all but are ignorant of the incongruence of these two ideas. Patriarchy is a system in which there can be no equality as it is based on a hierarchy with men at the apex. Since patriarchy itself is an illogical system for any person who truly believes in equal rights for all, using logical arguments will enable you to wear down fools who do not see the hypocrisy in their belief systems. One cannot honestly believe in equality while supporting an inequality-based system. Pointing this out to fools will likely need to be done over and over and will cause them cognitive dissonance and discomfort. Try to be patient and give them time to reconcile their worldview.

On the other hand, you will undoubtedly run into people who will admit they don't believe in equal rights for all. These people understand that patriarchy is a hierarchical system built on the idea that men are more worthy of power than women (as well as others who do not fit into the man-woman dichotomy). These people are assholes. You must also argue with all the assholes. Unfortunately, assholes are more challenging to persuade than fools because they don't have conflicting thought systems to exploit. To win the battle with an asshole, you will need to undermine their entire worldview. This will take a lot of work because you will have to use logic and facts upon facts that disprove their way of thinking.

You will also stumble upon religious zealots who defend the patriarchy with vigor. These people do so because they believe that is what their faith requires. These people are sheep. You must argue with all the sheep. Sheep don't have a logical thought process behind their ideology. This is not to say that all religious people are sheep. Many members of religious communities think logically about the history and culture of the time in which their religion was founded. These people embrace religious principles without perpetuating the biases and inequalities that have historically been a part of their religion. On the other hand, sheep do not think critically about their religion.

Sheep believe what religious leaders or their religious texts tell them without question. They assume the patriarchal system is divine, so you cannot argue against it. Also, they often subscribe to multiple logical fallacies. For example, they use the "appeal to authority" fallacy as they believe "God" is the ultimate moral authority. They also like to use the "bandwagon" fallacy. They will often claim their views are valid simply because many people agree with them (there are

2.3 billion Christians worldwide and 1.8 billion Muslims).[25] They will also try to "appeal to tradition" since their religion has been around for thousands of years. Lastly, they will use "circular thinking," saying that a particular thing is moral or immoral simply because they believe it to be so. Try to use logic and facts against them; some may be persuadable. It will be an uphill battle, but we must fight. Good luck.

---

[25] Hackett and McClendon, *Christians remain world's largest religious group, but they are declining in Europe.*

I see Trump and MAGA bumper stickers, flags, shirts, hats, signs, and banners everywhere I look. I see "Don't Tread on Me" and Confederate flags. I see QAnon, Oath Keepers, NRA (National Rifle Association), 2nd Amendment, guns, guns, and more guns. Right-wing extremism is VISIBLE! They are making themselves heard and seen, and politicians are taking notice. It is time for progressive, freedom-loving Americans to make themselves seen and heard. We need to drown out the drumbeat of the far right with rainbows and green (for abortion rights) everywhere. We must wear pro-choice and BLM (Black Lives Matter) t-shirts and hats. We need to fly LGBTQIA (lesbian, gay, bisexual, transgender, queer/questioning, intersex, and asexual) flags and plaster our cars with bumper stickers. We need to show up in the same way MAGA people have. We must be loud and proud and demand that politicians and other Americans listen to us. We have to stop shying away from displaying our political views.

I feel this would be an appropriate time to digress and ensure I explain the connection between the patriarchy and conservative, right-wing organizations. It is not news that American society, and before that European society, has historically been patriarchal. After all, the 19th Amendment, which granted women the right to vote, was not ratified until 1920. The first woman did not join Congress until 1917.[26] And still, in 2022, we have never had a female elected to the Presidency. However, the idea of patriarchy goes deeper than just the power difference between men and women. Patriarchy, at least in the United States, also has to do with the power difference between "men," as the framers of our Constitution defined them, and other groups such as African Americans, Native Americans, other minorities, and members of the LGBTQIA community. This can be seen in the fact that black men were not allowed to vote until the 15th Amendment was ratified in 1870 (94 years after the country's founding) and that discrimination against non-white people continues today. Not to mention, same-sex marriage was not federally recognized as legal in our country until 2015.[27] The brand of patriarchy found in the U.S. is concerned with maintaining the power of white, heterosexual, and mainly Christian men. To be sure, patriarchy takes many forms and appears differently in other areas of the world, but in this book, we will deal with American patriarchy.

Now that we have established the historical nature of patriarchy in America, let's talk about conservatism.

---

[26] History, Art & Archives, *Women in Congress.*

[27] Human Rights Campaign, *The Journey to Marriage Equality in the United States.*

conservatism (noun)

con·ser·va·tism | \ kən-ˈsər-və-ˌti-zəm \

Definition of *conservatism*

1 *capitalized*
a: the principles and policies of
a Conservative party
b: the Conservative party

2 a: disposition in politics to preserve what is
established
b: a political philosophy based on tradition and
social stability, stressing established institutions,
and preferring gradual development to abrupt
change

specifically **:** such a philosophy calling for lower
taxes, limited government regulation of business
and investing, a strong national defense, and
individual financial responsibility for personal
needs (such as retirement income or health-care
coverage)

3: the tendency to prefer an existing or traditional
situation to change
// religious *conservatism*
// cultural *conservatism*[28]

As you can see from the definition above, the very nature

of conservatism is to keep things as they've been in the past.

---

[28] Merriam-Webster, *Conservatism Definition & Meaning*.

This tendency serves the patriarchy as they are America's historical leaders and power holders. The right's tendency toward tradition and religion as a basis for moral authority acts as a stalwart barrier to changes that would shift the balance of power away from the traditional holders: the patriarchy.

Getting back to my original point, I'm sure you've heard the right call themselves "the moral majority." There's an assumption by Republicans that most people in the U.S. agree with their sense of morality. However, there's evidence that this isn't factual. In 2016, for example, 2,868,519 more people voted for Hillary Clinton than Donald Trump.[29] According to a Pew Research poll reported in June of 2022, 61% of Americans supported abortion rights in "all or most cases."[30] So why does the far-right believe they represent the majority of Americans?

A significant reason is that far-right beliefs are more visible in public. When people see the same information repeatedly, they are more likely to believe it to be true. This phenomenon is called the illusory truth effect.[31] The prominence of right-wing messages in the public eye then has

---

[29] The New York Times, *2016 Presidential Election Results*.

[30] Hartig, *About six-in-ten Americans say abortion should be legal in all or most cases.*

[31] Hassan and Barber, *The effects of repetition frequency on the illusory truth effect.*

two effects. The first is to make people believe that most Americans agree with these messages. The second is to convince people that the conservative viewpoint is a valid and acceptable way to think about the world.

This means we must work to make our perspectives public, visual, and omnipresent. When Americans go to the grocery store, I want them to be inundated with messages that the people around them support women's right to abortion. When they walk down the street, I want them to see that all their neighbors support gay marriage. When they go out to dinner, I want them to see that the patrons around them support BLM's message that we still have a lot of work to do to bring about equality in the U.S. Be bold and let people in your community know where you stand. The more people we can get to do this, the more often conservatives will see these messages and begin to internalize them, and the more social pressure we will put on them to change their worldviews. You must put your politics on full display in your community.

Leverage Social Media

While the messages we display on our person, cars, and homes will significantly affect our community, social media can allow us to reach a wider audience. Whether you use Facebook, Instagram, Twitter, TikTok, or all of the above, you need to put them to use spreading our message. Fill the internet with messages of solidarity against the patriarchy. Use these platforms to advance logical ideas, supported with facts, as to why you believe the right to privacy is a human right. Explain to people why you believe abortion is healthcare and why the right to gay marriage is a moral imperative. You need to respond, in real-time, to news stories and comments by politicians. You need to use this platform to argue, argue, argue. Argue with all the fools and assholes and sheep. Argue with them all.

You must also ensure that your social media accounts do not become a progressive echo chamber. The people you need to reach are not those who already agree with you. Make sure to interact with people whose worldview differs from yours. Ensure that you have conservative friends on Facebook. Follow and engage with conservatives on Twitter. Welcome arguments from the right; you can disprove them with logic and facts. Seek out those different from you and engage them respectfully and logically. To make a difference in this fight, you must invest time and energy in spreading your message and defending it with logic, reason, and facts. Every argument won is a victory in the war against the patriarchy.

Protest!

The First Amendment to the Constitution states, "Congress shall make no law respecting an establishment of religion, or prohibiting the free exercise thereof; or abridging the freedom of speech, or of the press; or the right of the people peaceably to assemble, and to petition the Government for a redress of grievances." Make use of your First Amendment rights! The people's right to speak out publicly against injustice is one of the cornerstones of our democracy. Attending rallies and protests will not only benefit our movement but will also benefit you personally. Protesting is a great way to let your anger and frustration out (remember Rule 3: uncork your rage). It also allows you to network with like-minded individuals and feel a sense of camaraderie with others in the movement. Seeing with your own eyes that you are not alone in the war can also re-energize feelings of hope and give you momentum to keep grinding away at the patriarchy, battle by battle.

Public protests are a physical, visual, and audible way to demand change. They are difficult for people to ignore. Of course, the more people involved, the stronger the message sent to our leaders and other politicians around the country. The sight and sound of thousands of people using their bodies and voices to communicate a united message can be a powerful catalyst for change. Join rallies and protests as often as you can. Ensure you focus your message on a solid argument. Stay peaceful, and remember that logic and truth are your weapons, not violence. Make sure to bring all your friends!

Dust Off Your Grammar Skills

You need to write. Write to your local newspaper. Drafting an opinion article will give you space to express more fully formed and informed arguments. Having your ideas published in a newspaper will also lend them credibility and give you a platform to reach a different audience than the one you regularly communicate with through social media. Publish your ideas in your local paper as often as you can.

You must also write to your elected representatives. Tell your state's senators and representatives in Congress what changes you want to see. Write to your governor and your state legislature. Demand they take action to protect Americans' human rights. Lay out arguments specific to your community or state and give them local facts supporting your point of view. Encourage other like-minded people to write their own letters, or let them sign on to yours to show their agreement. Although, I would say 30 individual letters making the same argument in different ways is more potent than 30 signatures on one letter. But either one will leave an impact.

Lastly, create and sign petitions for ballot initiatives or referendums. An example of the use of petitions would be to change your state's constitution to protect abortion rights specifically. Twenty-six states allow citizens to create initiatives or referendums on their ballots.[32] Another way you can use a petition is to push representatives to act in a particular manner (for example, petitioning to have Congress impeach Clarence Thomas). Websites such as change.org or thepetitionsite.com can help reach a broad audience. However, going door to door to get physical signatures, while much more time and energy-consuming, does have the upside of giving you a chance to speak to people in your community face-to-face. In-person interactions are always more meaningful and persuasive than online interactions. Create petitions, get out into your community, and spread your point of view.

---

[32] Ballotpedia, *States with Initiative or Referendum*.

Canvassing

Promote politicians who will help us take down the patriarchy. We must increase the number of government officials, from the city to the federal level, who believe in freedom and equality for all. We need leaders in the government who will fight for Americans' right to privacy, our right to bodily autonomy, and our right to travel freely. We need leaders who will actively participate in our fight against the patriarchy. We must be present and active in our communities to make this happen. You must volunteer to help political campaigns that espouse your viewpoint. I realize many people's ability to commit time to such things is limited, but canvassing can be highly impactful, even if it's only for one morning. Go door to door and let people in your community know that an election is around the corner. You can also canvas via telephone. Voice-to-voice communication is still more powerful than online communication. Talk to people about the virtues of your chosen candidate. Explain to them how voting for this candidate will help to ensure freedom for all Americans and how your candidate will benefit them personally. People supporting the fall of the patriarchy must speak face-to-face with people not yet on board. Don't avoid confrontation; you have logic, reasoning, and truth on your side. Get out there and convince your community to vote for candidates who will help us disassemble the patriarchy and ensure the freedoms enshrined in our Constitution become accessible to all.

CHAPTER FOUR

Slay Negative Stereotypes

One of the most powerful tools used by the patriarchy to maintain its power is stereotypes. Stereotypes inform people's implicit biases and play into fools' ability to maintain competing worldviews without realizing it. Stereotypes also serve to reinforce both assholes' and sheep's viewpoints.

implicit bias (noun)

im·plic·it | \ im-'pli-sət \ bi·as | \ 'bī-əs \
Plural: implicit biases

Definition of *implicit bias*

: a bias or prejudice that is present but not consciously held or recognized
// These studies reveal that students, nurses, doctors, police officers, employment recruiters, and many others exhibit *implicit biases* with respect to race, ethnicity, nationality, gender, social status, and other distinctions.
— J. T. Jost et al.
// "Research shows that the majority of people have an *implicit bias* that associates science and technology with gender, so from a very young age, girls are not encouraged to pursue these careers," she [Caroline Simard] said.
— Claire Cain Miller[33]

---

[33] Merriam-Webster, *Implicit Bias Definition & Meaning.*

People are generally unaware of their implicit biases. These hidden prejudices are informed by our day-to-day interactions and the information we gather from our environment, beginning when we are babies. We are sent the message over and over that women are weak and vain, men are strong and capable, women are victims, men are heroes, homosexuality is immoral, heterosexuality is the norm, black people are criminals, white people are victims, and so on. We all tend to internalize those ideas. In turn, these harmful ideas inform how we view the people around us and how we view ourselves. We've recognized this phenomenon since "The Doll Test" was presented as evidence in Brown v. Board of Education.[34] This test showed that both white and African American children chose to play with white baby dolls over black baby dolls. Again we see that repetitive messages have the power to change people's thinking and, in this case, cause a strong negative association.

When an entire society adopts a negative stereotype about a particular group, it can be challenging for that group to evade the adverse consequences of that stereotype. For example, the implicit bias of hiring managers can keep people from

---

[34] Legal Defense Fund, *A Revealing Experiment Brown v. Board and "The Doll Test."*

obtaining jobs that don't fit the stereotype of their group. As such, a gay man might find it challenging to get a job as a mechanic, or a woman might find it difficult to move into a leadership position within her company. Even in 2022, only 15% of CEOs in Fortune 500 companies are women.[35] Another example is the over-representation of minorities in crime statistics, which shows implicit bias affects police officers' actions on our streets. In 2019, the FBI reported that 29.9% of people arrested for curfew or loitering law violations were African American,[36] despite making up only about 14% of the population.[37] These are only a few examples, but I think they illustrate how stereotypes help keep power consolidated in the hands of those who are stereotyped in positive ways: the patriarchy.

These stereotypes hold such sway because we are inundated with messages that support them daily. We see these messages in movies, the news, and commercials and hear them at work and when hanging out with friends and family. Everywhere we turn, the messaging is consistent. Traditional narratives are being blasted loud and clear, but also in subtle

---

[35] Buchholz, *How has the number of female CEOs in Fortune 500 companies changed over the last 20 years?*
[36] Criminal Justice Information Services Division, *2019 Crime in the United States*, table 43A.
[37] Tamir et al., *Facts About the U.S. Black Population.*

ways that we cannot easily see for what they are. The patriarchy controls Hollywood, Disney, news outlets, the government, and in many cases, our families. Their message is the one getting through.

There are also many everyday things that people in our society say that have roots in negative stereotypes. For example, it's common for men to call someone a "pussy" if they believe the person to be weak or cowardly. Let's think about that for a moment. What group of people have pussies? Oh yeah, women. So, the assertion is that the person in question is similar to a woman, referring to the stereotype that women are the weaker sex and need men to stand up for them. When this proxy for womanhood is thrown around casually day in and day out as an insult, it has a detrimental effect on women's and girls' self-esteem. It also harms men's attitudes toward women. It perpetuates a negative stereotype that keeps the patriarchy in control.

Some people argue that "dick" is also used as a way to insult people. Let's look more deeply at that idea. The word "dick" is used to insult a person who mistreats others or breaks social norms. "Bitch" and "cunt" are sometimes used similarly to "dick" when directed toward women. However, as soon as those words are directed toward a man, they have an entirely different meaning. If a woman is a "bitch," she is forceful, insensitive, and demanding. If a man is a "bitch," he is weak and cowardly. Any time femininity is projected onto a man, it is considered an insult. This demonstrates that the feminine, the very essence of womanhood, at its core, is negative. To be like a woman is to be less than or insulted. This has to change.

I've heard plenty of women bolster negative stereotypes of women as well. I have frequently heard women discuss that they would much rather be friends with men because women are too catty, spiteful, or dramatic. Besides the fact that this is a pathetic attempt of weak-minded women to ally themselves with the patriarchy to gain favor, it also serves to preserve negative female stereotypes, all while dividing us and enabling the patriarchy to maintain the upper hand. It's ridiculous that we have to defend women's interests against other women, but it's the sad reality of our society.

Another way some women undermine their own equality is by participating in beauty pageants. This example is probably unnecessary, but I'm going to justify it as an example that I, myself, also follow the rules of how to nourish your sanity (notably Rule 3: uncork your rage). The entire point of a beauty pageant is to be judged on how pretty you are and how eloquently you can parade and flaunt your looks in front of an audience. Traditionally, beauty has been one of the most essential traits for a woman to possess. Our worth has primarily been based on men's desire for us. I argue that any woman who participates in or supports beauty pageants is doing herself and all women a great disservice. She is perpetuating the notion that women are objects to be admired and longed for by men. She is furthering the conception that women have no inherent value but only become valuable when men deem them a prize to be won. I, personally, rail against beauty pageants any chance I get. I hope you will take up this battle alongside me.

Let's get back to examples of everyday speech that further negative stereotypes. Lately, the trend of codifying homophobia and transphobia seems to be returning. A prime example is Florida's "Parental Rights in Education" bill (also known as the "Don't Say Gay" bill), in which teachers are prohibited from discussing sexual orientation or gender identity until after third grade.[38] Of course, these issues only come up when a person deviates from what is considered to be the norm. I've heard this bill defended by parents who say it's inappropriate for young children to learn about sexual orientation or gender identity. However, this is just code for, "I don't want my kid learning about non-conforming sexual and gender identities." The underlying assumption is that those

---

[38] Ron DeSantis Staff, *Governor Ron DeSantis Signs Historic Bill to Protect Parental Rights in Education.*

identities are immoral, and we should shield our children from them for as long as possible. Children are immersed in information about sexual orientation and gender identities from the time they're born. They see men kissing women on television and in the streets. They see men and women holding hands. They see families headed by a father and a mother. They see men and boys wearing pants. They see women and girls wearing skirts and dresses. They go to stores and see the "girls'" toy aisle full of dolls and dishes and pretend cleaning supplies, while the "boys'" toy aisle is full of dinosaurs and cars and Nerf guns. The patriarchy wants to keep instruction on these topics out of the younger grades to keep children from questioning these norms. They want children to internalize views of morality based on patriarchal, conservative Christian teachings. You must work to change people's underlying assumptions about the LGBTQIA community.

Another phrase I hear pretty regularly is, "Not to be racist, but were they black?" First, if you have to preface a statement with the words, "not to be racist," you're probably about to say something racist and should rethink your underlying assumptions. The last time I ran into this phrase, I was talking to an acquaintance about some unruly kids in Walmart. Her response to my story was the aforementioned phrase. We all carry implicit bias, every one of us. It's our job to personally recognize our biases, analyze the assumptions they're based on, and then correct our thinking accordingly. However, we cannot stop there. If people around you are unwilling, or perhaps unable, to check their assumptions, then it's up to you to stand up and question their biases for them. You must be part of the opposition to such thinking.

These are all examples of stereotypical speech that come up in day-to-day conversations. One of the many battles you will fight in waging this war against the patriarchy is confronting people who express ideas that prop up these negative stereotypes. Face-to-face confrontations can be uncomfortable, but they are necessary. Whether the person speaking is your coworker, friend, boyfriend, or mom, you must point out the assumptions that are the foundation of their comments. You have to question whether they genuinely believe those underlying assumptions. You must push them to see the harm in their words. You have to show them that their line of thinking is illogical and detrimental to the group they are stereotyping.

Of course, you will succeed more if you manage to have these conversations in private, but sometimes you need to call someone out publicly. In those times, you'll probably be labeled a troublemaker or "one of those girls," or they may call you a "bitch." Stay strong. This label is one more stereotype used to keep you down. Be "That Bitch." Take that title and fucking own it. Only when you take control of your self-image, confront bias unapologetically, and raise your voice to be heard will you become a slayer of negative stereotypes.

CHAPTER FIVE
Be Choosy

We are consumers of social messages. These messages are delivered to us through the music we listen to, the shows and movies we watch, and the books and magazines we read. These media are reflections of the society in which we live. However, they are also catalysts either for conservation of social values or for social change. The entertainment industry runs on capitalist principles. Therefore, it is responsive to consumers' demands. As entertainment media consumers, we choose what we listen to, watch, or read. These choices determine which types of messages dominate the industry. The entertainment industry has been slowly changing its messages to include more empowered women and more representations of minorities and the LGBTQIA community. However, patriarchal views are still dominant.

In this chapter, I want to look specifically at the music industry, which is notorious for objectifying women. We are portrayed as objects to be admired and acquired, which keeps us from being seen as full humans with thoughts, dreams, and ambitions of our own. Imagery objectifying women is rampant in many genres. Men, women, and kids listen to music daily, often without realizing its underlying message. Those messages are internalized without us even knowing it. Ask someone to recite a book they just read, and they will look at you like you're crazy. But, when a tune comes on the radio, we can sing it word for word with no problem. Without realizing it, the messages in our music permeate our memory and inform our thought processes.

Country music lyrics are rife with imagery of women as objects of entertainment for men. For example, in Luke Bryan's song, "Drunk on You," he sings: "Dancin' on the tailgate in a full moon, that kinda thing makes a man go mmm hmmm, you're lookin' so good in what's left of those blue jeans." Later in the song he says, "If you ain't a ten, you're a 9. 9." Luke Bryan bases all the woman's value on her looks and how much her dancing pleases him. He has the nerve to rate her on a one to ten scale as if he and other men are the arbiters of women's worth. After he decides she's good-looking enough, he says, "Let's slip on out where it's a little bit darker, and when it gets a little bit hotter, we'll take it off on out in the water." Luke knows what he wants but never considers what the woman might want. The entire song is about a man's wants and desires, which the woman is there to serve. She seems to be there for the sole purpose of the man's enjoyment.

Frank Ray's, "Country'd Look Good on You," might be even worse. He starts by singing about how much he likes this woman's looks. "You look good in them lights, you look good in them heels, you look good in that dress you got dressed up in to kill, you look good sippin' that wine behind that velvet rope, but damn, I'd love to see you on an old back road, I bet country'd look good on you." The implications of these lyrics are, first, that the woman is there for the man's pleasure and, second, that she should dress "country" to please him all the more. Next, he says he wants to take her to the middle of nowhere (not creepy at all) so he can fuck her. "If I get to lovin' on you like I want to, I bet country'd look good on you." Then, to reiterate his desires, he sings, "talkin' blanket in the bed underneath them pines, once we get out there, girl, we gon' stay out there all night, full moon shinin' on you, night sky so clear, get you where I want you 'cause it ain't in here." All he cares about is what *he* wants. He assumes this woman, the object of his desires, has no desires of her own. He assumes she has nothing better to do than spend the night in the woods with him, making all *his* dreams come true. Frank then bargains with the woman to get her to sleep with him. He says, "I'd let you steal my heart," and, "let you wake up in my shirt." He seems to think she should feel privileged to be his toy for the night. Then, to top it off, he describes how he thinks she should dress to make herself more appealing to him. "I'm talkin' faded blue jeans and cowgirl boots, an old snapback and my hands too." This song assumes that women exist to please men and that men are entitled to women's time and bodies.

The denigration of women is also present in pop music. In

the song, "Without You," The Kid LAROI sings about how upset he is after his lover leaves him. He says, "fuck all your reasons, I lost my shit, you know I didn't mean it." His words show he has no regard for how this woman feels or what she wants. He also refuses to take responsibility for "losing his shit," and seems to think she should just forgive him. Then, he insults her by repeatedly singing, "can't make a wife out of a ho, oh." This is a common trope in America's Puritan-based social ideology. Women in our society are often shamed if they have had multiple sex partners or are even suspected of having multiple partners. In this way, women can be controlled and forced to stay with their partner, often at the detriment of the woman's emotional, or sometimes physical, well-being. This system of thought is based on the idea that women exist to be owned by men. A woman who has had multiple sex partners has been "owned" by many men, which decreases her value in society's eyes.

Post Malone's "Psycho" lyrics are even more demeaning to women. After bragging about all his money, he then boasts about his sexual exploits. "I'm hittin' lil' mama, she wanna have my babies. It's fifty on the pinky, chain so stanky. You should see the whip, promise I can take yo' bitch. Boolin' with a thot-thot, she gon' give me top-top. Just one switch, I can make the ass drop." He shows no respect for these women or their feelings and assumes they exist for his gratification. He says he's, "boolin," or hanging out with a "thot." This is another term used to insult women who are considered promiscuous and actually stands for "that hoe over there." Then he claims she's going to give him "top," or head, and brags about how fast he can make her "ass drop," meaning get her to have sex with him. Post Malone seems more than willing to enjoy these women's sexual favors but then disparages them for the same behavior he exhibits. Later in the same song, he says, "had so many bottles, gave ugly girl a sip." This demonstrates that he only values women based on their looks. If you can believe it, this song was a number one hit on "Billboard Hot 100" in June of 2018.[39]

Beyond the objectifying imagery of our music, the voices we hear are overwhelmingly male. The BBC reported that in 2019 there were three times more male pop stars than females.[40] Research from 2019 shows that of the top 500 country songs between 2014 and 2018, only 16% were sung by women.[41] The fact that we're constantly listening to music that

---

[39] Trust, *Post Malone's "Psycho" Hits No. 1 on Billboard Hot 100, Maroon 5's "Girls Like You" Leaps to Top Five.*
[40] Youngs, *Pop Music's Growing Gender Gap Revealed in the Collaboration Age.*
[41] Annenberg Inclusion Initiative, *No Country for Female Artists: Artist & Songwriter Gender on Popular Country Charts from 2014 to 2018,* 1.

views the world through the male perspective is a problem for women and men. For women, it can be a lonely experience to listen to music that rarely reflects the world as you see it. To be constantly inundated with the male worldview can make you question yourself and your experiences. It can make you feel like no one else sees things the way you do, so perhaps your perspective is wrong.

On the other side, it makes it all the easier for men to ignore the female perspective. If they're rarely exposed to women's worldview, then it's easy to pretend it doesn't exist. It's easy to justify the objectification of women when they never hear any voices speaking out against it or expressing its effects.

The overwhelming male perspective in our music reflects that males dominate our society. They get the top jobs, make more money, make our laws, enforce our laws, and have a place of privilege in our homes, where they can enjoy their nice, clean house and not have to contribute to its maintenance. The constant objectification of women in our music results in the continuation of women's subjugation. As long as we are seen as nothing more than something pretty to look at, we can never be seen as people who have feelings and dreams of our own. As long as we are portrayed as existing for the sole purpose of entertaining and satisfying men, we can never be acknowledged for our personal talents and accomplishments.

As long as we are seen as objects to be owned, we can never be equals in American society.

We must force the music industry to promote female voices and perspectives by demanding music written and sung by women. We must put our money where our mouth is and support female artists by buying their albums. We must turn our backs on artists who disrespect women by refusing to listen to or purchase their music. We must teach our children that songs that denigrate women are unacceptable by turning the station when they are played on the radio. Consumers drive the music industry. Be choosy when listening to music, and we can slowly but steadily stamp out the patriarchal voices that influence our society.

CHAPTER SIX
Embrace and Defend

The war against the patriarchy is going to be long and arduous. If we are to be successful, we must all be clear not only on what we are fighting against but also on what we are fighting for. The war against patriarchy is the war for equality. Audre Lorde wrote in an essay in 1981, "I am not free while any woman is unfree, even when her shackles are very different from my own. And I am not free as long as one person of Color remains chained. Nor is any one of you."[42] The intent behind this quote is that none of us is free while any group of people is denied that same freedom. Equality exists when everyone has the same freedoms that other people have. Equality exists when everyone enjoys the same protection under the law. If you take on this mission, you must embrace and defend all groups of people against the tyranny of the patriarchy. These groups include not only women and African Americans but also Native Americans, other minorities, immigrants, and people in the LGBTQIA community, as well as any other groups that may be suffering at the hand of the patriarchy. If you don't embrace all these groups, your arguments for equality become as illogical as the patriarchy's.

While we are on this topic, I would like to address the current elephant in the room. There's a concerted effort by the

---

[42] Lorde, *The Uses of Anger*, 5.

right to turn women against transwomen by using the topics of bathroom access and sports to paint transwomen as predators coming to prey on girls and take away ciswomen's hard-fought rights. We are better than this. The underlying assumption behind the complaint about transwomen using women's bathrooms is that they are sexual predators. That's simply untrue. Period. As for whether or not transwomen have an advantage over ciswomen in sports, genetic variation among people is so wide-reaching that it's challenging to argue that because a transwoman was assigned male at birth, she automatically has an advantage over all other women. There are plenty of women in this world who are stronger than the majority of men. A 2015 study showed that the level of running performance for transwomen against ciswomen was consistent with the individuals' running performance against their male peers before transitioning.[43] A study in the British Journal of Sports Medicine in 2021 showed that transwomen competing at the Olympic level likely lose their physical advantage over ciswomen within two years of transition.[44] Let's put data aside; this comes down to whether or not we are willing to accept

---

[43] Kornei, *This scientist is racing to discover how gender transitions alter athletic performance-including her own.*

[44] Avery, *Trans women retain athletic edge after a year of hormone therapy, study finds.*

transwomen as women. A transwoman is a woman. She is my sister. She is your sister. She is our ally. Embrace her and her struggle.

Divide and conquer is an age-old strategy employed throughout history for one group to maintain control and power over other groups. Women, LGBTQIA individuals, African Americans, and other minorities must all see their struggle against the patriarchy as one and the same. You must see all people as equals. You must come to the defense of all people. You must work with, and for, all groups for us to successfully dismantle the patriarchy's power structure. These people are your allies.

Men, including heterosexual white men, can also be allies. Audre Lorde's concept can apply to men as well. No human is free, while another human is unfree. Many men understand this and want to fight the patriarchy alongside us. Embrace and defend them. Everyone who fights those in power incurs personal costs along the way. These men are no different. By joining the fight for equality, they risk becoming objects of ridicule by those who support the patriarchy. You must embrace and defend these men as allies.

I am a feminist to the core, but I have purposely steered away from discussing feminism in this book because I do not want any ally to be excluded from this fight.

feminism (noun)

fem·i·nism | \ ˈfe-mə-ˌni-zəm \

Definition of *feminism*

: belief in and advocacy of the political, economic, and social equality of the sexes expressed especially through organized activity on behalf of women's rights and interests[45]

While many feminists will tell you that feminism's premise is equality for all people, in many people's minds feminism focuses on only one aspect of the war against the patriarchy (the battle for power between the sexes). We will not be successful if we keep our focus so narrow. Ignoring our allies' struggles would be detrimental to our cause. Our war is one and the same. We have to stop seeing ourselves and our battles as separate. We are fighting for equality. If that word is not applied to every person, then it applies to none. Feminism is a limiting belief system. I believe men and women should be equal. But I also think trans women should be equal to men, black women should be equal to white women, gay men should be equal to cis men, and so on. You must break out of the feminist worldview and look at the issue more widely.

---

[45] Merriam-Webster, *Feminism Definition & Meaning.*

The stereotypes and biases that keep the patriarchy in control are deeply entrenched in our society. This war will be won one heart and one mind at a time. Turn no one away. You must recognize that every person is worthy of dignity and respect and every person deserves equality. Any person who believes this is your ally in this war and should be defended as you would defend yourself. Your mission is not only to convert as many people as you can into allies but also to embrace and defend all allies and their causes.

CHAPTER SEVEN
Put Your Money Where Your Mouth Is

In a capitalist society, money talks. Economic power is a significant hurdle to stamping out the patriarchy. When a government and society systematically deny a group of people access to economic opportunity, it significantly limits that group's ability to bring about social and political change. Let's first talk about how specific groups are denied economic opportunities. Then, we'll discuss how this translates into difficulty in bringing about change and what you can do to fight the patriarchy despite their superior economic power.

Women are denied economic opportunities in a multitude of ways. First, we shoulder a disproportionately large share of the domestic workload. According to a 2020 Institute for Women's Policy Research study, women spend two hours more on housework/care work than men daily.[46] That adds up to 730 hours a year of unpaid time that women cannot use in a way that benefits their health or careers. In 2021 The Center for Global Development released results from a study that showed that during the COVID-19 pandemic, women in high-income countries, such as the U.S., spent an additional 114

---

[46] Hess et al., *Providing Unpaid Household and Care Work in the United States: Uncovering Inequality*, 2.

hours more than men on taking care of children.[47] Add that to the 730 hours a year of extra work women were already doing, and we have a total of 844 hours women spent on domestic responsibilities. If we divide 844 hours into eight-hour work days, then women worked an average of 105.5 days more than men worked last year. That's 105.5 work days that men were able to use to further their careers, enjoy a hobby, or work on their health. That's 105.5 days that women spent taking care of housework and family. Accordingly, women have less time and energy to devote to careers and other passions and interests. For example, a mom who gets her kids ready for school in the morning, makes them breakfast and lunch, ensures they brush their teeth, works an entire eight-hour shift, picks up the kids from school, helps them with their homework, makes dinner, does the dishes, bathes the kids, sweeps the kitchen and then brushes the kids' teeth and puts them to bed, essentially has no time in her schedule to do anything extra to further her career. In that non-stop schedule, when would she find time to take college classes, begin writing a novel, or prepare for a presentation she has to give the next day at work? Most moms will tell you they do those things after

---

[47] Kenny and Yang, *The Global Childcare Workload from School and Preschool Closures During the COVID-19 Pandemic.*

their kids go to bed. That means that women are giving up the time they would be using to exercise, sleep, or take a moment to themselves to relax to do what little they can to get ahead in their careers.

Women cannot maintain a healthy lifestyle and a career simultaneously, and the amount of extra time they can commit to their careers is limited. This is, of course, not the case for all women, but it is for many. On top of this, society understands that this is how many women live. Hence, there is a stereotype that women, especially those with families or who plan to have families, are not as devoted to their careers. This negative stereotype then affects which positions and promotions are open to women. The Bureau of Labor and Statistics reports that surgeons and airline pilots are some of the top-earning occupations in the U.S.[48] Only 20.6% of general surgeons are women,[49] 8.05% of commercial pilots are women.[50] In 2021, the average compensation of chief executive officers (CEOs) of S&P 500 companies was $18.3 million.[51] Women only made

---

[48] U.S. Bureau of Labor and Statistics, *Occupational Outlook Handbook: Highest Paying Occupations.*

[49] Association of American Medical Colleges, *Physician Specialty Data Report: Active Physicians by Sex and Specialty, 2017.*

[50] Pilot Institute, *Women Pilot Statistics: Female Representation in Aviation.*

[51] Ockerman, *This is how much more an S&P 500 CEO earned than the typical worker last year.*

up 6.4% of CEOs in S&P 500 companies in 2021.[52] Women's perceived lack of dedication to their careers, coupled with other stereotypes (such as the idea that women don't make good leaders, they're too soft, too emotional, or too dramatic), also leads to substantial gaps in pay between men and women. 2019 U.S. Census Bureau data showed that women make 19% less money yearly than men.[53]

wealth (noun)

\ 'welth also 'weltth \

Definition of *wealth*

1: abundance of valuable material possessions or resources

2: abundant supply : profusion

3 a: all property that has a money value or an exchangeable value
b: all material objects that have economic utility

especially : the stock of useful goods having economic value in existence at any one time
// national wealth[54]

---

[52] Catalyst, *Women CEOs of the S&P 500.*
[53] Sheth et al., *These 8 charts show the glaring gap between men's and women's salaries in the US.*
[54] Merriam-Webster, *Wealth Definition & Meaning.*

The wealth gap between men and women is even more significant than the pay gap. A study by the Federal Reserve Bank of St. Louis discovered that the median wealth accumulation for families with female breadwinners was only 55 cents for every dollar accumulated by households headed by men.[55] Women work harder than men, yet we have less to show for our efforts.

Careers that women have historically dominated are also, despite their importance, undervalued and, therefore, underpaid. The average chemical engineer with a bachelor's degree makes $83,000 annually.[56] The average hourly wage for a nurse with a bachelor's degree is $31.38 per hour.[57] That's a yearly salary of around $65,000. The median public school teacher with a bachelor's degree makes between $51,762 and $57,260 per year, while a teacher with a master's degree makes a mere $52,444 to $58,167 per year.[58] American society expects women to work themselves to the bone for shitty pay out of the goodness of their hearts. They're supposed to sacrifice their time, sanity, health, and economic well-being in service to a society that does not appreciate them. In short,

---

[55] Hernandez, *Gender Wealth Gaps in the U.S. and Benefits of Closing Them.*

[56] Payscale, *Bachelor of Science (BS/BSc), Chemical Engineering Degree.*

[57] Payscale, *Average Registered Nurse (RN) Hourly Pay.*

[58] Salary.com, *Salaries for Public School Teacher with a Bachelor's Degree.*

women lack the time, energy, and resources to easily mount an attack on the patriarchal system that is actively keeping them from reaching their full potential.

Of course, women are not the only group suffering at the hands of the patriarchy. People in the LGBTQIA community have historically suffered from hiring and other types of discrimination. Statistics on income for people within this group vary widely from subgroup to subgroup and from study to study. Suffice it to say, we need more information to get an accurate picture. However, LGBTQ-economics.org reported that in 2017 gay men earned 32% less money than cismen, and lesbians earned 11% less than cis women.[59] Meanwhile, transexual people were four times more likely than the average person to have a yearly salary of less than $10,000.[60] No one can live off that. LGBTQIA people are suffering right along with us.

African Americans and other cultural minorities are also struggling economically. A 2020 report by the Board of Governors of the Federal Reserve System showed that the average amount of wealth for a white family in the U.S. is

---

[59] LGBTQ-Economics, *The LGBTQ Wealth Gap.*
[60] LGBTQ-Economics, *The LGBTQ Wealth Gap.*

$983,400.[61] Meanwhile, the average wealth for a black family is $142,500, and the average wealth of a Hispanic family is $165,500.[62] Furthermore, the U.S. Census Bureau reported in 2000 that 71% of white Americans owned their home, while only 56% of Native Americans, 45% of Pacific Islanders, and 46% of black and Hispanic Americans owned their homes.[63] The Census Bureau also reported that in 2019, 7.3% of white Americans lived below the poverty line. Comparatively, 15.7% of Hispanic Americans and 18.8% of African Americans lived in poverty.[64] This demonstrates the economic and social reality that is a consequence of the patriarchal system for non-white groups.

---

[61] Bhutta et al., *Disparities in Wealth by Race and Ethnicity in the 2019 Survey of Consumer Finances.*

[62] Bhutta et al., *Disparities in Wealth by Race and Ethnicity in the 2019 Survey of Consumer Finances.*

[63] United States Census Bureau, *Historical Census of Housing Tables: Homeownership by Race and Hispanic Origin.*

[64] Creamer, *Inequalities Persist Despite Decline in Poverty For All Major Race and Hispanic Origin Groups.*

Powerless

At the most basic level, people struggling to pay their bills do not possess the time, money, or energy to affect changes that would benefit them. They do not have money to donate to politicians who support their causes. They do not have time to volunteer for political campaigns. If you're someone who can't afford a car, it may be difficult for you to make it to a polling place to vote in elections. If all your time is spent working, cleaning, and caring for kids, you don't have time to follow politics. When you spend all your time figuring out how to pay your rent, the fact that the Supreme Court took away your bodily autonomy may not even be on your radar.

In 2016, only 48% of voters who earned $5000 per year or less participated in the presidential election, while about 66% of voters earning between $35,000 and $45,000, and 86% of voters earning between $125,000 and $150,000 participated.[65] In the 2020 presidential election, 65% of people with income in the bottom third voted, while 88% of the top third voted.[66] The discrepancy in voter turnout between low and high-income voters directly translates to less representation in the

---

[65] Akee, *Voting and Income.*

[66] Clemens, Lake, and Mitchell, *Evidence from the 2020 election shows how to close the income voting divide.*

government for people who need the government's protection most.

The patriarchy keeps as many as possible in a constant daily struggle to survive, so we don't have time or energy to worry about, or engage in, politics. Ignorance is not bliss. Whether you know it or not, the Supreme Court and many of our state governments are stripping your rights away from you. You will live with the consequences even if you have no clue what's happening right under your nose. Ignorance is powerlessness. Ignorance enables others to take advantage of you.

What You Can Do

Your mission is to lift as many people out of this state of ignorance and constant struggle as possible. Keep them informed; talk to them about important issues in their lives. If you are in a good economic position, do what you can to lift these people out of the poverty that constricts their political lives. If you're a business owner, do everything you can to give your employees a living wage. If your neighbor walks to the grocery store weekly, offer them a ride. If you're a lawmaker, enact laws that will decrease the wealth gap. What you can do in this regard is determined by your unique situation. Do what you can. Your challenge is to see everyone in your community as part of the solution to inequality. Lifting our neighbors out of poverty is one of the first steps in freeing our allies to join the war. The patriarchy wins as long as their energy is wasted battling for daily necessities. You must fight for economic justice for all and be willing to contribute however you can.

Whether we like it or not, we all contribute to the patriarchy's economic power. Most people shop where they can get the most bang for their buck or where it's convenient for them. This has led to companies like Amazon and Walmart dominating markets all over the U.S. and destroying small businesses. Their owners have amassed profane fortunes, with

Jeff Bezos (executive chairman and founder of Amazon) worth $136.8 billion,[67] and Rob Walton (heir of Sam Walton, who founded Walmart) worth $57.9 billion.[68] Hobby Lobby, which has refused to provide its employees with birth control coverage[69] and advocated for the U.S. to become a Christian theocracy,[70] has enabled its owner, David Green, to accumulate a net worth of $5.2 billion.[71] It's time for us to stop lining the patriarchy's pockets. Of course, there will be those who must sit this battle out. If you're someone who lives where the only grocery store around for miles is Walmart, and you don't have the means to go elsewhere, then Rule 4: pick your battles.

Those with the means must research the companies where they choose to spend their money. Shop at places that treat their employees well and align with your values. Spend at businesses owned by women and people in LGBTQIA or other minority groups. Don't get suckered in by Amazon's free shipping and convenience. Don't let Hobby Lobby's immense array of craft supplies be more important to you than fighting

---

[67] Taylor and Farkas, *How Much is Jeff Bezos Worth?*

[68] Garfinkle, *Who is Billionaire Rob Walton, the Likely Future Owner of the Denver Broncos?*

[69] FindLaw's Team of legal writers and editors, *The Hobby Lobby Case: Contraception and Religious Freedom.*

[70] Crump, *Hobby Lobby Faces Backlash Over Newspaper Ad Calling for Christian-Run Government.*

[71] Celebrity Net Worth, *David Green Net Worth.*

for equality. These companies have the power they do because we've given it to them. We can also take that power away.

Below are some websites that can help you make informed decisions about where to shop. Keep abreast of news on this front and create your own website, Facebook page, etc., to help people in your community determine where they can best spend their hard-earned money.

- https://donegood.co/blogs/news/boycott-trump-companies-to-avoid

- https://fortune.com/2022/06/30/companies-supporting-abortion-rights-roe-v-wade-first-movers/

- https://www.ethicalconsumer.org/ethicalcampaigns/boycotts

- https://theresponsibleconsumer.wordpress.com/products-to-boycott-test/

Another way you can financially support the war for equality is to donate. You can donate money. You can also donate time. Again, Rule 4: pick your battles. Not everyone can donate money, and not everyone can donate time. Do what you can. We need to support political candidates that will fight for equality. Donate money to these campaigns. Donate your time to canvass or create advertisements. You must support these campaigns.

Many organizations are fighting the patriarchy. Organizing

gives people a sense of community, camaraderie, and hope, and amplifies our voices. It is essential to support organizations that oppose the patriarchy. Some examples are the Center for Reproductive Rights, NARAL Pro-Choice America, ACLU, Human Rights Campaign, Planned Parenthood, Black Lives Matter, and Audre Lorde Project. Of course, many, many more organizations are doing this work. Find an organization that you believe in and donate either money or time. If you've got the time, you could organize your own local chapter of an organization or create your own from scratch. Find allies in your community who want to work toward equality in your area.

Face-to-face, local organizing can be a powerful force. There's plenty of anecdotal evidence that in-person communication is more effective than phone calls or emails. We've all experienced this personally. However, there are also data to back this up. A 2017 study in the Journal of Experimental Social Psychology showed that speaking with someone in person made it 34 times more likely that they would comply with your request.[72] Talking with people face-to-face is vital in our war against the patriarchy. We've got to

---

[72] Bohns, *A Face-to-FAce Request Is 34 Times More Successful Than an Email.*

get out there and speak with people in-person if we're going to be effective at persuading them to become allies. The heart of this war is individual, face-to-face battles with fools, assholes, and sheep. One by one, we have to work to convert them. You must support, either through monetary donations or volunteering your time, the organizations that are out there doing this work.

Many people fighting the patriarchy do not have money to donate to the cause. Still, others do not have time to volunteer to help this cause. A substantial portion of us also have neither time nor money and are struggling just to make it through the day. I realize this and am not suggesting they are not making significant contributions to this war. Each of us has to do what we can. We cannot ask any more than that of our allies. Having said that, many of us do have time and/or money to donate. To those allies, I say, put your money where your mouth is. Expand this to include your time, as time is money. You can leverage the precious resources of time and money to make a difference in the war for equality. We must pool our resources to support allies in our communities, political candidates, and organizations fighting battles against patriarchy. You must prioritize funding this war (with time, money, or both if you have it).

CHAPTER EIGHT
Take Your Time

As you're reading this book, you may wonder how on Earth you could find the time to do all of this. Don't freak out! Remember the rules for nourishing your sanity:

Rule 1: celebrate every triumph!
Rule 2: take breaks
Rule 3: uncork your rage
Rule 4: pick your battles

You don't have to do everything that I suggest in this book. I recommend that, for your own sanity, you don't…unless you have a whole lot of time, money, and patience on your hands. Then, by all means, fucking go for it! The rest of us will be pacing ourselves. This leads us to our most important resource in the war to demolish the patriarchy: time. As discussed in the previous chapter, women spend an average of 730 hours more than men per year doing unpaid domestic work.[73] I don't think that number surprises anyone reading this book. How can we fight the patriarchy when we barely have time to sleep? The answer is that we can't. Therefore, one of the most important battles you must wage against the patriarchy is to take back

---

[73] Hess et al., *Providing Unpaid Household and Care Work in the United States: Uncovering Inequality.*

your time. Time is money. Time is sanity. Time is health. Take it back.

Think of how great it would feel to sleep eight hours every night. What would it be like to put your feet up and watch the news while someone else does the dishes? You know you would knock that work presentation out of the park if you spent the evening before preparing for it. How would it feel to run every other morning while someone else makes the kids' lunches? How much better would your life be if you took all your chores, divided them in two, and handed half to someone else?

Sounds fantastic, doesn't it? This transformation takes time and may not be entirely possible for many of us, but it sure would be awesome. Unload what you can. It's time for men to start doing their part, and most will not willingly take on this burden. According to Pew Research Center, 46% of men believe they split housework evenly with their partner.[74] Obviously, they're delusional. A marriage therapist in Minnesota claims the complaint she often hears from women in couples therapy is that their partners are not actively

---

[74] Barroso, *For American couples, gender gaps in sharing household responsibilities persist amid pandemic*.

responsible for housework.[75] Most of us have experienced this type of person. Active responsibility is when you take it upon yourself to do what needs to be done, while passive responsibility is when you offer to help with whatever needs to be done, which puts ownership of the task onto the other person. This is why men feel that women are nagging them when they ask them to help around the house. They perceive housework as the woman's responsibility; they're just there to help you with *your* chores. And don't forget to say thank you and praise them for how wonderfully they did or good luck getting help next time. It's up to you to put your foot down. It's up to you to take your time.

I want to be clear, not all men are like this. But in my experience, most are. So, if you're in a relationship with this type of person, I have a few ideas to help you take back your time.

- Make a list of all the household chores, then sit down with him and split them in half by the amount of time they take

- Each of you makes a journal of all tasks you do around the house and notes how long you spend doing them—compare at the end of two weeks

---

[75] Robinson, *Marriage Therapist Reveals The Top Complaint From Women.*

- Make a journal of how much time your partner spends not doing chores, then demand the same amount of time for yourself

- If your partner is not willing to do their half (and you can't kick them to the curb)

  - split your home in half and tell them to stay on their side

  - Pick up anything they leave lying around the house, any dishes they don't clean, and any laundry they don't wash and pile it on their side of the bed

  - Don't clean anything-live in a pigsty until they give in

Demanding that your partner respects your time is not easy, but it's necessary. You deserve time to exercise, eat right, sleep, and relax. You deserve to have the time and energy left at the end of your day to read a book, work on a hobby, or fight the patriarchy. Beyond that, you are an example for your children, future children, and other people's children. We must demonstrate to all our daughters that women get to choose how they allow others to treat them. We must also show them what to do when they are not treated the way they want. We must demonstrate to all our sons and daughters how to treat their partners equitably. We will win the war against the patriarchy in our homes. We must change how future generations of men and women view equity and their responsibilities to one another. You must take back your time to set a good example.

If you are one of the many women struggling to make it day to day, reclaiming your time must be your top priority. If all your time and energy is spent working, cleaning, cooking, and caring for others, how can you possibly find the energy to argue with fools, destroy negative stereotypes, or volunteer for a political campaign? You can't. For that reason, you must make taking back your time your top priority. Only after you've won that battle can you join the other battles women are waging daily. You deserve equity, and you deserve respect, especially from the person who is closest to you, your partner. Our children deserve positive role models that teach them how to stand up for themselves and demand respect when it isn't given. The fight for time is essential. It comes before all other battles. You must take your time.

CHAPTER NINE
Vote!

If we are going to grind the dead bones of the patriarchy to dust and scatter them to the wind, you must vote! It's probably obvious, but voting at every level is essential if we are to defeat the patriarchy. Our democracy cannot continue if we allow the patriarchy to take human rights away from vast portions of American citizens. A country with significant wealth gaps between rich and poor and a government that does not protect the rights of large parts of the population will eventually fall into chaos. There's only so much people can take before they revolt. We have to restore the rule of law to the United States. We need equality in this country in order to have a fully functioning democracy. Americans need to know their human rights are protected and they will be treated equally under the law. To accomplish this, we have to have a voice in the laws and policies of our country. The more local, state, and federal candidates we can elect, the louder our voices will be.

Donald Trump and Republicans in Congress packed the Supreme Court with extreme religious fanatics. The officials we elect to the federal government can have far-reaching effects not only by writing laws and setting policies but also by deciding whether or not our fundamental human rights will be respected and protected. The recent example of the overturning of Roe v. Wade shows how important federal elections are. However, many smaller local and state elections contributed to

Republicans having the power to appoint these zealots to the highest court in the land.

Local officials have a massive influence on which citizens have the time, energy, and money to contribute to the war against the patriarchy. Local officials determine zoning laws, which impact which parts of the community will suffer the health consequences of being near factory pollution. Local officials decide where and when bus lines will run, which affects mobility from one part of a city to another. They choose where voting locations will be, which affects how difficult it is for residents to vote (particularly those who rely on public transportation). Local officials decide which businesses get city contracts and where developers can build apartments in the city. Local officials also decide what our children will learn at school, which helps determine their attitudes toward diversity, inclusion, and equality (not to mention logic and reasoning skills). Local officials' decisions affect people's quality of life, education, ability to access city resources, and ability to exercise their right to vote. You must vote in local elections.

State officials, of course, control state laws but also how state and federal elections are run. State laws can take away any right not protected by the constitution. In the wake of the Dobbs decision, state after state has passed severely restrictive abortion laws. Beyond that, however, state legislatures are in charge of drawing voting districts. This gives them tremendous power in deciding how much your vote counts. There are two ways legislatures can gerrymander the voting map. The first is to draw voting districts to split a voting group into multiple districts so they can't elect their preferred candidate in any district. The second is to pack all the people of one voting group into as few districts as possible to limit the number of candidates they can elect. Either way, it removes the power of the gerrymandered groups' votes. This can keep people, even if they represent a majority, from electing candidates that will fight for their causes. State legislatures can also determine how difficult it is for specific groups to vote. They can set limits on mail-in voting and decrease the availability of mail ballot drop boxes. They decide where election locations will be and how long they will be open, which can lead to long lines in some areas and make it difficult for shift workers to vote. In 2021, Georgia even made it illegal to give food or water to someone standing in line to vote.[76] State officials can significantly affect your ability to exercise your human rights and your power to elect state and federal representatives that will fight for your beliefs. You must vote in state elections.

---

[76] Wilder and Baum, *5 Egregious Voter Suppression Laws from 2021.*

You must vote in every single election. Make sure those around you know when and how to vote. Give people rides to vote. Talk to people about which candidates you think will do the most to fight the patriarchy and work toward equality in America. Although women make up over half the U.S. population, the House of Representatives of the 117th Congress was 27% women, while the Senate was only 24% women.[77] On top of this, white Americans make up 60% of the population but 77% of Congress.[78] We cannot defeat the patriarchy while they run the government that makes the rules we all have to play by. You must vote in ALL elections.

---

[77] Blazina and Desilver, *A record number of women are serving in the 117th Congress.*
[78] Schaeffer, *Racial, ethnic diversity increases yet again with the 117th Congress.*

CHAPTER TEN
Fuck the Patriarchy

This is war. The patriarchy is coming for your unalienable rights. They wish to deprive you of the right to "Life, Liberty, and the pursuit of Happiness," enshrined in the Declaration of Independence. They are forcing women to have babies in a nation where our maternal mortality rate is higher than any other industrialized nation.[79] The Common Wealth Fund reported that the U.S. ranked 11th among 11 industrialized nations on health care outcomes.[80] The Supreme Court stripped us of our right to terminate a pregnancy and the right to control our bodies and destinies. The United States no longer recognizes the right to privacy or bodily autonomy.

The patriarchy is now trying to rob us of the ability to keep from getting pregnant in the first place. On July 21st, 2022, the House of Representatives voted on a bill to affirm the right of Americans to access contraceptives. Out of 213 Republicans in the house, 195 voted against the bill.[81] Only a handful of days before that, 205 out of 213 Republicans voted against a bill to protect women's right to interstate travel for abortion[82] The

---

[79] Tikkanen et al., *Maternal Mortality and Maternity Care in the United States Compared to 10 Other Developed Countries*.

[80] Schneider et al., *Mirror, Mirror 2021: Health Care in the U.S. Compared to Other High-Income Countries*.

[81] Mccann Ramirez, *All But 10 House Republicans Voted Against Ensuring the Right to Contraception*.

[82] Bensen, *Nearly every GOP rep rejects bill to protect interstate abortion travel*.

patriarchy views women as incubators for men to use as they please. Fuck the patriarchy.

The patriarchy is using the government to scare and intimidate women into submission. In 2016, when Chris Matthews (a reporter with MSNBC) asked Donald Trump if women should be punished for abortion, Trump stated, "The answer is that there has to be some form of punishment."[83] Matthews clarified, "For the woman," and Trump responded, "Yeah, there has to be some form."[84] Later in the interview, Trump reiterated, "I have not determined what the punishment would be."[85] Trump has announced that he is running for the presidency in 2024. Senator Ted Cruz supports banning abortion even when pregnancy results from rape, saying, "As horrible as that crime is, I don't believe it's the child's fault. And we weep at the crime, we want to do everything we can to prevent the crime on the front end, and to punish the criminal, but I don't believe it makes sense to blame the child."[86] Although he won't say it, Cruz is advocating punishing *women*

---

[83] Kertscher, *In Context: Transcript of Donald Trump on punishing women for abortion.*

[84] Kertscher, *In Context: Transcript of Donald Trump on punishing women for abortion.*

[85] Kertscher, *In Context: Transcript of Donald Trump on punishing women for abortion.*

[86] Opoien, *Ted Cruz in Wisconsin: Roe v. Wade not settled, ban abortion with no exceptions.*

for their rapists' deeds as well. Making it illegal to abort rapists' fetuses forces women into enduring nine months of torture as their rapists' DNA spreads and grows against their will within their bodies. Nor has Cruz considered the predicament these women will face once their rapists' babies are born. In September of 2022, Senator Lindsey Graham proposed a federal abortion ban after 15 weeks of gestation, except for rape or incest, and if the mother's life is in danger.[87] So much for Republicans' claims that abortion is an issue for the states to decide. If they have their way, women will have to leave the country to get an abortion, as well as routine medical care for miscarriages. Then, when women return, the government will investigate them for murder so the patriarchy can punish them.

The patriarchy is also using shame to force women into submission. Representative Matt Gaetz recently tried to bully women into staying home so they couldn't exercise their 1st Amendment right to speak out against the patriarchy's tyranny. In July of 2022, at a Student Action Summit in Florida, Gaetz called women who attend pro-choice rallies "disgusting" and railed, "Why is it that the women with the least likelihood of

---

[87] Allen, Caputo, and Wong, *'Bad idea': Republicans pan Lindsey Graham's 15-week abortion ban.*

getting pregnant are the ones most worried about having abortions? Nobody wants to impregnate you if you look like a thumb."[88] He also seethed, "These people are odious on the inside and out. They're like 5'2, 350 pounds, and they're like, 'Give me my abortions, or I'll get up and march and protest.'"[89] Gaetz's contempt for women is astounding. He is an elected representative for the state of Florida. That man has a hand in making laws that affect women nationwide. He is blatantly trying to silence women so the patriarchy can maintain control.

If the government can force us to risk our lives to give birth and force us to carry our rapists' fetuses, then women are the ones who do not have a right to life. If we can't control our bodies or travel freely about the country, then we do not have liberty. If we can't decide whether to have a child, then we do not have the right to pursue happiness. Fuck the patriarchy.

On top of the patriarchy's assault on women, they are now trying to take away marriage equality. Justice Clarence Thomas's concurring opinion in the Dobbs decision stated that the court should reconsider all precedents based on the 14th

---

[88] Jones, *A Texas teen raises over $700,000 for abortions after Rep. Matt Gaetz mocked her.*

[89] Jones, *A Texas teen raises over $700,000 for abortions after Rep. Matt Gaetz mocked her.*

Amendment's Due Process Clause.[90] That clause protects not only the constitutional right to contraception but also the right to same-sex marriage and to do as you please in your bedroom. On July 19th, 2022, 157 House Republicans voted against the Respect for Marriage Act, which would have codified the right to same-sex marriage if it had become law.[91]

Even though fundamental human rights are not up for debate, Republicans such as Senators Ted Cruz[92] and Josh Hawley[93] have been advocating for letting individual states decide whether all Americans are entitled to equal marriage rights. Other Republicans are outright attacking the LGBTQIA community in an effort to divide and conquer. In May of 2022, Representative Marjorie Taylor Greene claimed that trans people are "targeting our kids" and that trans people wanting to play sports and use the restroom is "trans-terrorism."[94] Senator John Cornyn has even insinuated that allowing

---

[90] Thomas, *Thomas E. Dobbs, State Health Officer of the Mississippi Department of Health, et al., Petitioners v. Jackson Women's Health Organization, et al.*, 119.

[91] Rodriguez, *The House Passed the Respect for Marriage Act. 157 Republicans Voted Against It.*

[92] Diaz, *Ted Cruz says Supreme Court was 'clearly wrong' about 2015 same-sex marriage ruling.*

[93] Desrochers, *Hawley opposes bill to protect same-sex marriage, says the issue should be left to the states.*

[94] Hamilton, *WATCH: MTG slams 'trans-terrorism' and says 'leave our kids alone. Let them grow up.'*

LGBTQIA people to marry whom they choose would infringe on the right of Christians to practice their religion.[95] Republicans are pitting the LGBTQIA community against women and Christians, using lies to frighten enough people in these groups to keep them from uniting on issues like abortion access and marriage equality. They're using LGBTQIA people as pawns in their game to divide and conquer without a care for the consequences.

Conservative leaders' negative attitudes toward the LGBTQIA community, which became even more acceptable under the Trump presidency, have also had physical consequences. The Center for the Study of Hate and Extremism-CSUSB (California State University, San Bernadino) found that between 2014 and 2019, hate crimes against gay men increased by 24.54%, and hate crimes against transgender people increased by 160.34% across the nation.[96] The right to live your life in safety is a human right. Choosing who you love and how you love them is a human right. Human rights should never be up for debate. Fuck the patriarchy.

---

[95] Levy, *Republican Senator Lashes Out at Marriage Equality in Supreme Court Hearing.*

[96] CSUSB, *FACT SHEET: Anti-Asian Prejudice March 2021 Center for the Study of Hate & Extremism, 4.*

Violence against non-white Americans is also a longstanding part of American history and continues to this day. It is a powerful weapon in the patriarchy's arsenal. Between 2014 and 2019, hate crimes against African Americans increased by 19.06% nationwide.[97] Meanwhile, Republican leaders, such as Senator Ted Cruz, claim Black Lives Matter (BLM) is a terrorist organization.[98] In 2020 Rudy Giuliani, former Mayor of New York City and lawyer to Donald Trump, also called BLM "a domestic terrorist group" and stated that the people in the organization "are killers, and these are people who hate white people. They're people who hate white men in particular. And they want to do away with a mother-father family."[99] The patriarchy disparages African American organizations and labels them terrorist groups to undermine their legitimacy and foment more violence against them.

The patriarchy uses the same tactic against other minority groups. In 2015, Donald Trump defended his call to keep Muslims from entering the U.S., saying, "our country cannot

---

[97] CSUSB, *FACT SHEET: Anti-Asian Prejudice March 2021 Center for the Study of Hate & Extremism*, 4.

[98] Sharp, *Senator Ted Cruz calls riots 'organized terror attacks', slams Black Lives Matter protesters as 'avowed Marxists' and blasts Democrats for 'letting cities burn' ahead of his Antifa hearing.*

[99] Deese, *Giuliana says Black Lives Matter is 'domestic terrorist' group.*

be the victims of horrendous attacks by people that believe only in Jihad, and have no sense of reason or respect for human life."[100] From 2018 to 2019, hate crimes against Arabs increased by 15.85%.[101] Yet, when Representative Ilhan Omar sponsored a bill in 2021 to fight against anti-Muslim sentiments in the U.S., Representative Scott Perry accused her of being "affiliated" with terrorist organizations.[102]

In 2016, Trump spoke of Mexican immigrants saying, "They're bringing drugs. They're bringing crime. They're rapists. And some, I assume, are good people."[103] Reporters also revealed in 2019 that Trump privately said that he wanted the southern border wall to be "electrified" and have "spikes on top that could pierce human flesh."[104] Between 2014 and 2019, hate crimes against Hispanics increased by 76.25%.[105]

During 14 days in March of 2020, Trump referred to the

---

[100] Taylor, *Trump Calls For 'Total And Complete Shutdown of Muslims Entering' U.S.*

[101] Deese, *Giuliana says Black Lives Matter is 'domestic terrorist' group.*

[102] Weisman, *Republican Rebuked for Anti-Muslim Remarks in 'Islamophobia' Debate.*

[103] Scott, *Trump's most insulting-and violent-language is often reserved for immigrants.*

[104] Scott, *Trump's most insulting-and violent-language is often reserved for immigrants.*

[105] CSUSB, *FACT SHEET: Anti-Asian Prejudice March 2021 Center for the Study of Hate & Extremism, 4.*

COVID-19 virus as the "Chinese virus" more than 20 times.[106] He continued throughout his presidency to call COVID-19 names like the "Wuhan virus" and "kung flu." The president of the United States purposely associated a deadly virus with Chinese people. The Federal Bureau of Investigation found that in one year, from 2019 to 2020, hate crimes against Asians increased by 77%.[107] The organization Stop AAPI Hate reported that from March 2020 to June 2021, they received 9,081 reports of violence against Asians.[108]

The Anti-Defamation League found that white supremacist organizations in the U.S. nearly doubled their efforts at spreading propaganda between 2019 and 2020 (this included passing out posters, banners, fliers, and stickers with racist, anti-LGBTQIA, and anti-Semitic messages).[109] We are in a pandemic of hate sewn by the patriarchy. They spread this disease to sever us from our allies. Divided, we are weak, and they know it. Fuck the patriarchy.

The ideas, systems, and institutions that keep us

---

[106] Viala-Gaudefroy and Lindaman, *Donald Trump's 'Chinese virus': the politics of naming.*

[107] Findling, *COVID-19 Has Driven Racism And Violence Against Asian Americans: Perspectives From 12 National Polls.*

[108] The Associated Press, *More Than 9,000 Anti-Asian Incidents Have Been Reported Since The Pandemic Began.*

[109] ADL, *White Supremacist Propaganda Spikes in 2020.*

imprisoned by the patriarchy are woven into the fabric of American society. They are present every day in many subtle ways. They exist in our language. They exist in our interactions. They exist in our thought processes. To defeat the patriarchy is an impossible mission. You, yourself, will never see it come to fruition. We will win this war by microscopic degrees. When the tide turns in our favor, it will be undetectable. To think this way can be overwhelming, but it can also be empowering. One raindrop cannot sustain a forest; it takes them all. Countless numbers of raindrops must fall, or the forest will perish. You are a raindrop. Alone, you are insignificant, but together we can sustain the movement for equality. We can bring down on the patriarchy a mighty tsunami to wipe it from our shores. Be the earthquake whose ripples send the tidal wave steadily and imperceptibly building into a massive, unstoppable force to strike down our oppressors and restore the balance of power amongst the people. Fuck the patriarchy.

Works Cited

ACLU. *Abortion in Texas*. ACLUTexas.org (August 29, 2022) Accessed
     November 8, 2022. https://www.aclutx.org/en/know-your-
     rights/abortion-texas.

ADL. *White Supremacist Propaganda Spikes in 2020*. ADL (May 3, 2022).
     Accessed October 4, 2022. https://www.adl.org/white-
     supremacist-propaganda-spikes-2020.

Akee, Randall. *Voting and Income*. EconoFact (February 7, 2019).
     Accessed September 20, 2020. https://econofact.org/voting-and-
     income.

Allen, Jonathan, Marc Caputo, and Scott Wong, *'Bad idea': Republicans
     pan Lindsey Graham's 15-week abortion ban*. NBC News
     (September 13, 2022). Accessed November 3, 2022.

Annenberg Inclusion Initiative. *No Country for Female Artists: Artist &
     Songwriter Gender on Popular Country Charts from 2014 to
     2018*. USC Annenberg Inclusion Initiative (2019). Accessed
     October 5, 2022. 1. https://assets.uscannenberg.org/docs/no-
     country-for-female-artists-research-brief_2019-04-04.pdf.

Association of American Medical Colleges. *Physician Specialty Data
     Report: Active Physicians by Sex and Specialty, 2017* (December
     2017). Accessed October 5, 2022. https://www.aamc.org/data-
     reports/workforce/interactive-data/active-physicians-sex-and-
     specialty-2017.

Autry, Blake M. and Roopma Wadhwa. *Mifepristone*. National Library of
     Medicine (May 8, 2022). Accessed October 4, 2022.
     https://www.ncbi.nlm.nih.gov/books/NBK557612/#:~:text=Mifep
     ristone%20is%20a%20synthetic%20steroid,competitively%20bin
     ding%20its%20intracellular%20receptor.

Avery, Dan. *Trans women retain athletic edge after a year of hormone
     therapy, study finds*. NBC News (January 5, 2021). Accessed
     September 3, 2022. https://www.nbcnews.com/feature/nbc-
     out/trans-women-retain-athletic-edge-after-year-hormone-
     therapy-study-n1252764.

Bahari, Sarah. *Texas woman nearly died from infection because doctors could not perform legal abortion*. The Dallas Morning News (October 20, 2022). Accessed November 8, 2022. https://www.dallasnews.com/news/texas/2022/10/19/texas-woman-nearly-died-from-infection-because-doctors-could-not-perform-legal-abortion/.

Ballotpedia. *States with Initiative or Referendum*. Ballotpedia. Accessed on September 25, 2022. https://ballotpedia.org/States_with_initiative_or_referendum.

Barroso, Amanda. *For American couples, gender gaps in sharing household responsibilities persist amid pandemic*. Pew Research Center (January 25, 2021). Accessed October 4, 2022. https://www.pewresearch.org/fact-tank/2021/01/25/for-american-couples-gender-gaps-in-sharing-household-responsibilities-persist-amid-pandemic/#:~:text=A%20majority%20of%20women%20(59,spouse%20or%20partner%20does%20more.

Bensen, Steve. *Nearly every GOP rep rejects bill to protect interstate abortion travel*. MSNBC (July 18, 2022). Accessed October 4, 2022. https://www.msnbc.com/rachel-maddow-show/maddowblog/nearly-every-gop-rep-rejects-bill-protect-interstate-abortion-travel-rcna38694.

Bhutta, Neil, Andrew C. Chang, Lisa J. Dettling, and Joanne W. Hsu. *Disparities in Wealth by Race and Ethnicity in the 2019 Survey of Consumer Finances*. Board of Governors of the Federal Reserve System (September 28, 2020). Accessed September 16, 2022. https://www.federalreserve.gov/econres/notes/feds-notes/disparities-in-wealth-by-race-and-ethnicity-in-the-2019-survey-of-consumer-finances-20200928.html.

Blazina, Carrie and Drew Desilver. *A record number of women are serving in the 117th Congress*. Pew Research Center (January 15, 2021). Accessed October 4, 2022. https://www.pewresearch.org/fact-tank/2021/01/15/a-record-number-of-women-are-serving-in-the-117th-congress/.

Bohns, Vanessa. *A Face-to-FAce Request Is 34 Times More Successful Than an Email*. Harvard Business Review (April 11, 2017). Accessed October 2, 2022. https://hbr.org/2017/04/a-face-to-face-request-is-34-times-more-successful-than-an-email.

Bryan, Luke. *Drunk on You.* Genius.com (February 2012). Accessed October 30, 2022. https://genius.com/Luke-bryan-drunk-on-you-lyrics.

Buchholz, Katharina. *How has the number of female CEOs in Fortune 500 companies changed over the last 20 years?* World Economic Forum (March 10, 2022). Accessed August 29, 2022. https://www.weforum.org/agenda/2022/03/ceos-fortune-500-companies-female/#:~:text=Fortune%20500%20companies.-,As%20of%20March%2C%20there%20were%2074%20female%20CEOs%20employed%20at,the%20country's%20biggest%20public%20businesses.

Catalyst. *Women CEOs of the S&P 500* (July 12, 2022). Accessed October 30, 2022. https://www.catalyst.org/research/women-ceos-of-the-sp-500/.

Celebrity Net Worth. *David Green Net Worth*. Celebrity Net Worth (2022). Accessed September 15, 2022. https://www.celebritynetworth.com/richest-businessmen/richest-billionaires/david-green-net-worth/.

Clemens, Austin, Shanteal Lake, and David Mitchell. *Evidence from the 2020 election shows how to close the income voting divide*. Washington Center for Equitable Growth (July 8, 2021). Accessed October 12, 2022. https://equitablegrowth.org/evidence-from-the-2020-election-shows-how-to-close-the-income-voting-divide/.

Cornell Law School. *Dobbs v. Jackson Women's Health Organization*. Legal Information Institute (June 24, 2022). Access August 29, 2022. https://www.law.cornell.edu/supremecourt/text/19-1392.

Creamer, John. *Inequalities Persist Despite Decline in Poverty For All Major Race and Hispanic Origin Groups*. United States Census Bureau (September 15, 2020). Accessed September 20, 2020.

https://www.census.gov/library/stories/2020/09/poverty-rates-for-blacks-and-hispanics-reached-historic-lows-in-2019.html.

Criminal Justice Information Services Division. *2019 Crime in the United States*. FBI: UCR (2019). Accessed August 29, 2022. Table 43A. https://ucr.fbi.gov/crime-in-the-u.s/2019/crime-in-the-u.s.-2019/tables/table-43.

Crump, James. *Hobby Lobby Faces Backlash Over Newspaper Ad Calling for Christian-Run Government*. Newsweek (July 5, 2021). Accessed September 17, 2022. https://www.newsweek.com/hobby-lobby-christian-july-4-advert-1606873.

CSUSB. *FACT SHEET: Anti-Asian Prejudice March 2021 Center for the Study of Hate & Extremism*. CSUSB (2020). Accessed October 4, 2022. https://www.csusb.edu/sites/default/files/FACT%20SHEET-%20Anti-Asian%20Hate%202020%20rev%203.21.21.pdf.

Deese, Kaelan. *Giuliana says Black Lives Matter is 'domestic terrorist' group*. The Hill (August 6, 2020). Accessed October 31, 2022. https://thehill.com/homenews/media/510953-giuliani-says-black-lives-matter-is-domestic-terrorist-group/.

Desrochers, Daniel. *Hawley opposes bill to protect same-sex marriage, says the issue should be left to the states*. St. Louis Post-Dispatch (September 8, 2022). Accessed October 31, 2022. https://www.stltoday.com/news/local/govt-and-politics/hawley-opposes-bill-to-protect-same-sex-marriage-says-the-issue-should-be-left-to/article_b9822497-bad4-53f4-a8f9-9979a84880be.html.

Diaz, Daniella. *Ted Cruz says Supreme Court was 'clearly wrong' about 2015 same-sex marriage ruling*. CNN Politics (July 19, 2022). Accessed October 31, 2022. https://www.cnn.com/2022/07/17/politics/ted-cruz-same-sex-marriage-supreme-court/index.html.

Drukker L, E Bradburn, GB Rodriguez, NW Roberts, L Impey, and AT Papageorghiou. *How Often Do We Identify Fetal Abnormalities during Routine Third-Trimester Ultrasound? A Systematic Review and Meta-Analysis*. BJOG: An International Journal of

Obstetrics & Gynaecology 128, no. 2 (2020): 259–69. Accessed
July 30, 2022. https://doi.org/10.1111/1471-0528.16468.

Durkee, Alison. *Overturning Roe v. Wade: Here's How Abortion Bans Will
Hurt State Economies and the GDP*. Forbes. Forbes Magazine
(June 25, 2022). Accessed June 27, 2022.
https://www.forbes.com/sites/alisondurkee/2022/06/25/overturnin
g-roe-v-wade-heres-how-abortion-bans-will-hurt-state-
economies-and-the-gdp/?sh=2de9e92f3c6d.

FindLaw's Team of legal writers and editors. *The Hobby Lobby Case:
Contraception and Religious Freedom*. FindLaw (November 18,
2018). Accessed September 17, 2022.
https://www.findlaw.com/family/reproductive-rights/the-hobby-
lobby-case-contraception-and-religious-freedom.html.

Findling, Mary, Robert J. Blendon, John Benson, and Howard Koh.
*COVID-19 Has Driven Racism And Violence Against Asian
Americans: Perspectives From 12 National Polls*. HealthAffairs
(April 12, 2022). Accessed October 4, 2022.
https://www.healthaffairs.org/do/10.1377/forefront.20220411.655
787/.

Finer, Lawrence B., Lori F. Frohwirth, Lindsay A. Dauphinee, Susheela
Singh, and Ann M. Moore. *Reasons U.S. Women Have
Abortions: Quantitative and Qualitative Perspectives.
Guttmacher Institute*. Perspectives on Sexual and Reproductive
Health 37, no. 3 (September 1, 2005): 110-118. Accessed
September 3, 2022.
https://www.guttmacher.org/journals/psrh/2005/reasons-us-
women-have-abortions-quantitative-and-qualitative-perspectives.

Garfinkle, Madeline. *Who is Billionaire Rob Walton, the Likely Future
Owner of the Denver Broncos?* Entrepreneur (June 8, 2020).
Accessed September 15, 2022.
https://www.entrepreneur.com/business-news/who-is-rob-walton-
see-his-net-worth-and-denver-broncos-
deal/429123#:~:text=What%20is%20Rob%20Walton's%20net,ri
chest%20person%20in%20the%20world.

Goodwin, Michele. *How the Criminalization of Pregnancy Robs Women of
Reproductive Autonomy*. "The Hastings Center Report"

(November 24, 2017). Wiley Online Library. Accessed October 4, 2022. https://onlinelibrary.wiley.com/doi/full/10.1002/hast.791.

Hackett, Conrad and David McClendon. *Christians remain world's largest religious group, but they are declining in Europe*. Pew Research Center (April 5, 20147). Accessed September 18, 2022. https://www.pewresearch.org/fact-tank/2017/04/05/christians-remain-worlds-largest-religious-group-but-they-are-declining-in-europe/.

Hamilton, Heather. *WATCH: MTG slams 'trans-terrorism' and says 'leave our kids alone. Let them grow up.'* The Denver Gazette (May 19, 2022. Accessed October 31, 2022. https://denvergazette.com/news/nation-world/watch-mtg-slams-trans-terrorism-and-says-leave-our-kids-alone-let-them-grow-up/article_e55df018-95af-5f27-8909-4732ab33eb85.html.

Hartig, Hannah. *About six-in-ten Americans say abortion should be legal in all or most cases*. Pew Research Center (June 13, 2022). Accessed September 15, 2022. https://www.pewresearch.org/fact-tank/2022/06/13/about-six-in-ten-americans-say-abortion-should-be-legal-in-all-or-most-cases-2/.

Hassan, Aumyo and Sarah J. Barber. *The effects of repetition frequency on the illusory truth effect*. Cognitive Research: Principles and Implications 6, no. 38 (May, 13, 2021). Accessed September 18, 2022. https://cognitiveresearchjournal.springeropen.com/articles/10.1186/s41235-021-00301-5.

Hernandez Kent, Ana. *Gender Wealth Gaps in the U.S. and Benefits of Closing Them*. Federal Reserve Bank of St. Louis (September 29, 2021). Accessed September 10, 2022. https://www.stlouisfed.org/open-vault/2021/september/gender-wealth-gaps-us-benefits-of-closing-them.

Hess, Cynthia Ph.D., Tanima Ahmed, M. Phil, and Jeff Hayes, Ph.D. *Providing Unpaid Household and Care Work in the United States: Uncovering Inequality*. Institute for Women's Policy Research (January 2020). Accessed November 3, 2022. chrome-extension://efaidnbmnnnibpcajpcglclefindmkaj/https://iwpr.org/w

p-content/uploads/2020/01/IWPR-Providing-Unpaid-Household-and-Care-Work-in-the-United-States-Uncovering-Inequality.pdf.

History, Art & Archives. *Women in Congress. United States House of Representatives*. Accessed September 1, 2022. https://history.house.gov/Exhibition-and-Publications/WIC/Women-in-Congress/#:~:text=Since%201917%2C%20when%20Representative%20Jeannette,%2C%20Resident%20Commissioners%2C%20or%20Senators.

Huff, Charlotte. *In Texas, Abortion Laws Inhibit Care for Miscarriages*. NPR (May 10, 2022). Accessed July 10, 2022. https://www.npr.org/sections/health-shots/2022/05/10/1097734167/in-texas-abortion-laws-inhibit-care-for-miscarriages.

Human Rights Campaign. *The Journey to Marriage Equality in the United States*. Human Rights Campaign. Accessed August 18, 2022. https://www.hrc.org/our-work/stories/the-journey-to-marriage-equality-in-the-united-states.

Jones, Dustin. *A Texas teen raises over $700,000 for abortions after Rep. Matt Gaetz mocked her*. NPR (July 28, 2022). Accessed November 3, 2022. https://www.npr.org/2022/07/28/1114300388/matt-gaetz-olivia-julianna-abortion-gen-z-for-change.

Kenny, Charles and George Yang. *The Global Childcare Workload from School and Preschool Closures During the COVID-19 Pandemic*. Center for Global Development (June 25, 2021). Accessed on September 12, 2022. https://www.cgdev.org/publication/global-childcare-workload-school-and-preschool-closures-during-covid-19-pandemic.

Kertscher, Tom. *In Context: Transcript of Donald Trump on Punishing women for abortion*. PolitiFact (March 30, 2016). Accessed November 2, 2022. https://www.politifact.com/article/2016/mar/30/context-transcript-donald-trump-punishing-women-ab/.

Kimball, Spencer. *Women in states that ban abortion will still be able to get abortion pills online from overseas.* CNBC (June 27, 2022). Accessed September 2, 2022. https://www.cnbc.com/2022/06/27/women-in-states-that-ban-abortion-will-still-be-able-to-get-abortion-pills-online-from-overseas.html.

Kornei, Katherine. *This scientist is racing to discover how gender transitions alter athletic performance-including her own.* Science (July 25, 2018). Accessed on August 27, 2022. https://www.science.org/content/article/scientist-racing-discover-how-gender-transitions-alter-athletic-performance-including.

LAROI, The Kid. *Without You.* Genius.com (November 6, 2020). Accessed October 30, 2022. https://genius.com/The-kid-laroi-without-you-lyrics.

Legal Defense Fund. *A Revealing Experiment Brown v. Board and "The Doll Test."* NAACP. Accessed August 18, 2022. https://www.naacpldf.org/brown-vs-board/significance-doll-test/.

Levy, Pema. *Republican Senator Lashes Out at Marriage Equality in Supreme Court Hearing.* Mother Jones (March 22, 2022). Accessed October 31, 2022. https://www.motherjones.com/politics/2022/03/john-cornyn-marriage-equality-ketanji-brown-jackson-supreme-court/.

LGBTQ-Economics. *The LGBTQ Wealth Gap.* LGBTQ-Economics (2019). Accessed August 29, 2022. https://lgbtq-economics.org/wp-content/uploads/2020/03/LGBTQ-Wealth-Gap-Summary.pdf.

Lorde, Audre. *The Uses of Anger.* City University of New York Academic Works: Women's Studies Quarterly. Accessed August 9, 2022. 5. https://academicworks.cuny.edu/cgi/viewcontent.cgi?article=1654&context=wsq.

Malone, Post. *Psycho.* Genius.com (February 23, 2018). Accessed October 30, 2022. https://genius.com/Post-malone-psycho-lyrics.

Mccann Ramirez, Nikki. *All But 10 House Republicans Voted Against Ensuring the Right to Contraception*. RollingStone (July 21, 2021). Accessed October 4, 2022. https://www.rollingstone.com/politics/politics-news/republicans-vote-against-right-to-contraception-bill-1386356/.

Merriam-Webster. *Conservatism Definition & Meaning*. Merriam-Webster. Accessed August 28, 2022. https://www.merriam-webster.com/dictionary/conservatism.

Merriam-Webster. *Feminism Definition & Meaning*. Merriam-Webster. Accessed October 30, 2022. https://www.merriam-webster.com/dictionary/feminism.

Merriam-Webster. *Implicit Bias Definition & Meaning*. Merriam-Webster. Accessed August 29, 2022. https://www.merriam-webster.com/dictionary/implicit%20bias#:~:text=%3A%20a%20bias%20or%20prejudice%20that,social%20status%2C%20and%20other%20distinctions.

Merriam-Webster. *Impossible Definition & Meaning*. Merriam-Webster. Accessed July 13, 2022. https://www.merriam-webster.com/dictionary/impossible.

Merriam-Webster. *Patriarchies Definition & Meaning*. Merriam-Webster. Accessed June 28, 2022. https://www.merriam-webster.com/dictionary/patriarchies.

Merriam-Webster. *Wealth Definition & Meaning*. Merriam-Webster. Accessed August 28, 2022. https://www.merriam-webster.com/dictionary/wealth#:~:text=Definition%20of%20wealth,value%20or%20an%20exchangeable%20value.

National Advocates for Pregnant Women. *Arrests and Prosecutions of Pregnant Women, 1973-2020*. National Advocates for Pregnant Women (September 18, 2021). Accessed October 1, 2022. https://www.nationaladvocatesforpregnantwomen.org/arrests-and-prosecutions-of-pregnant-women-1973-2020/.

Ockerman, Emma. *This is how much more an S&P 500 CEO earned than the typical worker last year*. MarketWatch (July 24, 2022). Accessed October 30, 2022. https://www.marketwatch.com/story/the-typical-s-p-500-ceo-made-324-times-more-than-the-median-paid-worker-last-year-report-11658253925.

Opoien, Jessie. *Ted Cruz in Wisconsin: Roe v. Wade not settled, ban abortion with no exceptions*. The Cap Times (April 4, 2016). Accessed November 2, 2022. https://captimes.com/news/local/govt-and-politics/election-matters/ted-cruz-in-wisconsin-roe-v-wade-not-settled-ban-abortion-with-no-exceptions/article_06c97918-d7b6-5727-b3e4-d5dd6d0123c5.html.

Paltrow, Lynn M. and Jeanne Flavin. *Arrests of and Forced Interventions on Pregnant Women in the United States, 1973–2005: Implications for Women's Legal Status and Public Health*. "Journal of Health Politics, Policy and Law" 38, no. 2 (April 1, 2013): 299–343. Accessed October 1, 2022. https://read.dukeupress.edu/jhppl/article/38/2/299/13533/Arrests-of-and-Forced-Interventions-on-Pregnant.

Payscale. *Average Registered Nurse (RN) Hourly Pay*. payscale. Accessed August 28, 2022. https://www.payscale.com/research/US/Job=Registered_Nurse_(RN)/Hourly_Rate.

Payscale. *Bachelor of Science (BS/BSc), Chemical Engineering Degree. Payscale*. Accessed September 18, 2022. https://www.payscale.com/research/US/Degree=Bachelor_of_Science_(BS_%2F_BSc)%2C_Chemical_Engineering/Salary.

Pilot Institute. *Women Pilot Statistics: Female Representation in Aviation*. Pilot Institute (February 22, 2022). Accessed September 27, 2022. https://pilotinstitute.com/women-aviation-statistics/.

Ray, Frank. *Country'd Look Good On You*. Genius.com (July 30, 2021). Accessed October 30, 2022. https://genius.com/Frank-ray-countryd-look-good-on-you-lyrics

Robinson, Gregory. *Marriage Therapist Reveals The Top Complaint From Women*. Tyla (May 16, 2022). Accessed October 4, 2022. https://www.tyla.com/sex-and-relationships/passive-responsibility-active-responsibility-corrinthecounselor-tiktok-20220516.

Rodriguez, Mathew. *The House Passed the Respect for Marriage Act. 157 Republicans Voted Against It.* them (July 20, 2022). Accessed October 4, 2022. https://www.them.us/story/the-house-passed-the-respect-for-marriage-act-157-republicans-voted-against-it.

Ron DeSantis Staff. *Governor Ron DeSantis Signs Historic Bill to Protect Parental Rights in Education*. Florida Governor's Office. Accessed October 5, 2022. https://flgov.com/2022/03/28/governor-ron-desantis-signs-historic-bill-to-protect-parental-rights-in-education/#:~:text=Governor%20Ron%20DeSantis%20Signs%20Historic%20Bill%20to%20Protect%20Parental%20Rights%20in%20Education,-On%20March%2028&text=SPRING%20HILL%2C%20Fla.,the%20upbringing%20of%20their%20children.

Salary.com. *Salaries for Public School Teacher with a Bachelor's Degree*. Salary.com (2022). Accessed August 28, 2022. https://www1.salary.com/Salaries-for-Public-School-Teacher-with-a-Bachelors-Degree.

Schaeffer, Katherine. *Racial, ethnic diversity increases yet again with the 117th Congress*. Pew Research Center (January 28, 2021). Accessed October 4, 2022. https://www.pewresearch.org/fact-tank/2021/01/28/racial-ethnic-diversity-increases-yet-again-with-the-117th-congress/.

Schneider, Eric C., Arnav Shah, Michelle M. Doty, Roosa Tikkanen, Katharine Fields, Reginald D. Williams II. *Mirror, Mirror 2021: Health Care in the U.S. Compared to Other High-Income Countries*. The Commonwealth Fund (August 4, 2021). Accessed October 4, 2022. https://www.commonwealthfund.org/publications/fund-reports/2021/aug/mirror-mirror-2021-reflecting-poorly#:~:text=The%20U.S.%20continues%20to%20outspend,countries%20compared%20in%20this%20report.

Scott, Eugene. *Trump's most insulting-and violent-language is often reserved for immigrants*. The Washington Post (October 2, 2019). Accessed November 3, 2022. https://www.washingtonpost.com/politics/2019/10/02/trumps-most-insulting-violent-language-is-often-reserved-immigrants/.

Scribner, Herb. *'Not Her Body, Not Her Choice': Indiana Legislature Passes near-Total Abortion Ban*. Axios, August 6, 2022. https://www.axios.com/2022/08/06/indiana-eric-holcomb-abortion-bill-vote.

Sharp, Rachel. *Senator Ted Cruz calls riots 'organized terror attacks,' slams Black Lives Matter protesters as 'avowed Marxists' and blasts Democrats for 'letting cities burn' ahead of his Antifa hearing*. Daily Mail (August 4, 2020). Accessed October 31, 2022. https://www.dailymail.co.uk/news/article-8591813/Senator-Ted-Cruz-calls-riots-organized-terror-attacks-ahead-Antifa-hearing.html.

Sheth, Sonam, Madison Hoff, Marguerite Ward, and Taylor Tyson. *These 8 charts show the glaring gap between men's and women's salaries in the US*. Insider (March 15, 2022). Accessed September 22, 2022. https://www.businessinsider.com/gender-wage-pay-gap-charts-2017-3.

Tamir, Christine, Abby Budiman, Luis Noe-Bustamante, and Lauren Mora. *Facts About the U.S. Black Population*. Pew Research Center (March 25, 2001). Accessed September 1, 2022. https://www.pewresearch.org/social-trends/fact-sheet/facts-about-the-us-black-population/#:~:text=The%20Black%20population%20of%20the,Black%20Americans%20are%20diverse.

Taylor, Jennifer and Jami Farkas. *How Much is Jeff Bezos Worth?* GoBankingRates (2020). Accessed September 15, 2022. https://www.gobankingrates.com/net-worth/business-people/jeff-bezos-net-worth/.

Taylor, Jessica. *Trump Calls For 'Total And Complete Shutdown of
        Muslims Entering' U.S.* NPR (December 7, 2015). Accessed
        November 3, 2022.
        https://www.npr.org/2015/12/07/458836388/trump-calls-for-
        total-and-complete-shutdown-of-muslims-entering-u-s.

The Associated Press. *More Than 9,000 Anti-Asian Incidents Have Been
        Reported Since The Pandemic Began.* NPR (August 12, 2021).
        Accessed October 4, 2022.
        https://www.npr.org/2021/08/12/1027236499/anti-asian-hate-
        crimes-assaults-pandemic-incidents-aapi.

The Commission on Presidential Debates. *October 19, 2016 Debate
        Transcript.* The Commission on Presidential Debates. Accessed
        August 15, 2022. https://www.debates.org/voter-
        education/debate-transcripts/october-19-2016-debate-transcript/.

The New York Times. *2016 Presidential Election Results.* The New York
        Times. Accessed August 27, 2022.
        https://www.nytimes.com/elections/2016/results/president.

Thomas, Clarence. *Thomas E. Dobbs, State Health Officer of the
        Mississippi Department of Health, et al., Petitioners v. Jackson
        Women's Health Organization, et al.* Supreme Court of the
        United States. Accessed June 24, 2022. 119.
        https://www.supremecourt.gov/opinions/21pdf/19-1392_6j37.pdf.

Tikkanen, Roosa, Munira Z. Gunja, Molly Fitzgerald, and Laurie Zephyrin.
        *Maternal Mortality and Maternity Care in the United States
        Compared to 10 Other Developed Countries.* The
        Commonwealth Fund (November 18, 2020). Accessed October 4,
        2022. https://www.commonwealthfund.org/publications/issue-
        briefs/2020/nov/maternal-mortality-maternity-care-us-compared-
        10-countries.

Trust, Gary. *Post Malon'es "Psycho" Hits No. 1 on Billboard Hot 100,
        Maroon 5's "Girls Like You" Leaps to Top Five.* Billboard (June
        11, 2018). Accessed on September 28, 2022.
        https://www.billboard.com/pro/post-malone-psycho-no-1-hot-
        100/.

U.S. Bureau of Labor and Statistics. *Occupational Outlook Handbook: Highest Paying Occupations*. United States Government (September 8, 2022). Accessed September 15, 2022. https://www.bls.gov/ooh/highest-paying.htm.

United States Census Bureau. *Historical Census of Housing Tables: Homeownership by Race and Hispanic Origin*. United States Census Bureau (2000). Accessed September 20, 2022. https://www.census.gov/data/tables/2000/dec/coh-ownershipbyrace.html.

Viala-Gaudefroy, Jerome and Dana Lindaman. *Donald Trump's 'Chinese virus': the politics of naming*. The Conversation (April 13, 2021). Accessed November 3, 2022. https://theconversation.com/donald-trumps-chinese-virus-the-politics-of-naming-136796.

WebMD. *Misoprostol-Uses, Side Effects, and More*. WebMD. Accessed October 2, 2022. https://www.webmd.com/drugs/2/drug-6111/misoprostol-oral/details.

Weisman, Jonathan. *Republican Rebuked for Anti-Muslim Remarks in 'Islamophobia' Debate*. The New York Times (December 14, 2021). Accessed November 3, 2022.

Wilder, Will and Stuart Baum. *5 Egregious Voter Suppression Laws from 2021*. Brennan Center For Justice (January 31, 2022). Accessed October 4, 2022. https://www.brennancenter.org/our-work/analysis-opinion/5-egregious-voter-suppression-laws-2021.

Youngs, Ian. *Pop Music's Growing Gender Gap Revealed in the Collaboration Age*. BBC News (February 19, 2019). Accessed on October 5, 2022. https://www.bbc.com/news/entertainment-arts-47232677.

Youth for Human Rights. *United Nations Universal Declaration of Human Rights*. Youth for Human Rights. Accessed August 25, 2022. https://www.youthforhumanrights.org/what-are-human-rights/universal-declaration-of-human-rights/introduction.html.

www.ingramcontent.com/pod-product-compliance
Lightning Source LLC
Chambersburg PA
CBHW020530160726
47992CB00005BA/2323